THE OXFORD BOOK OF
SHORT POEMS

The Oxford Book of
Short Poems

Chosen and Edited by
P. J. Kavanagh and James Michie

Oxford New York
OXFORD UNIVERSITY PRESS

Oxford University Press, Walton Street, Oxford OX2 6DP

Oxford New York Toronto
Delhi Bombay Calcutta Madras Karachi
Kuala Lumpur Singapore Hong Kong Tokyo
Nairobi Dar es Salaam Cape Town
Melbourne Auckland
and associated companies in
Beirut Berlin Ibadan Nicosia

Oxford is a trade mark of Oxford University Press

First published 1985
Reprinted 1985

British Library Cataloguing in Publication Data
The Oxford book of short poems.
1. English poetry
I. Kavanagh, P. J. II. Michie, James.
821'.008 PR1174
ISBN 0-19-214135-X

Library of Congress Cataloging in Publication Data
Main entry under title:
The Oxford Book of short poems.
1. English poetry. 2. American poetry.
I. Kavanagh,.P. J. (Patrick Joseph), 1931– II. Michie, James.
PR1175.95 1985 821'.008 84-27294
ISBN 0-19-214135-X

Set by Latimer Trend & Company Ltd.
Printed in Great Britain by
Richard Clay (The Chaucer Press), Ltd.
Bungay, Suffolk

CONTENTS

CONTENTS

CONTENTS

CONTENTS

CONTENTS

CONTENTS

CONTENTS

CONTENTS

xii

CONTENTS

CONTENTS

xiv

CONTENTS

CONTENTS

CONTENTS

CONTENTS

CONTENTS

CONTENTS

CONTENTS

CONTENTS

CONTENTS

xxiii

CONTENTS

CONTENTS

CONTENTS

CONTENTS

CONTENTS

xxviii

CONTENTS

CONTENTS

CONTENTS

CONTENTS

CONTENTS

CONTENTS

xxxiv

CONTENTS

XXXV

CONTENTS

INTRODUCTION

THIS collection of short poems (very short—less than fourteen lines, to avoid the sonnet which otherwise would have swamped it) has been made with the intention of seeing what new light such a limitation could throw on poetry as a whole: what poets and poems have been overlooked or treated ungenerously, and what short poems, even if they have been anthologized, have had their effect muffled by their longer companions. The idea has been to give short poems (which need not be short-winded poems) room to breathe. Besides, the short can be accessible, memorable and enjoyable.

Most general anthologies tend to pick the same poems. These are usually long, or longish, because it is presumed that poets are best represented at their most ambitious, which is not necessarily true; and the shorter poems are usually the same ones, by the same poets. Thus we are once again taken down what Seamus Heaney has called 'the motorway of English verse'. There have been collections of 'little known' or 'rare' poems of this or that century, but on the whole these turn out to be little known for good reason; to examine them is to leave the motorway to explore lanes and byways, which may be pleasant and instructive, but the main traffic trundles on unchanged. This anthology is an attempt to bring together the best that has been written, among poems below a certain length, from medieval times to the present day.

The attempt contained a fascination: for some reason poets, without necessarily being personal, often seem to reveal more of themselves, as writers and as individuals, and more of the flavour of their time, when they are writing briefly. Perhaps when they are being lengthy they feel the need to dress up more. So this turned out to be an introduction to poets, as well as to poems. Also, in brevity there can be a sudden perfection: Thomas Beedome, for instance, in the four lines of no. 79, or Anon in no. 180.

There was a sense of relief, too, in being able to give even well-known poets more opportunity to show their variety: Sir Thomas Wyatt, usually represented by the same anthology-pieces, Ben Jonson, a master of the short form, Thomas Campion, who brings depth and colour to the already rich convention of Elizabethan songs, Robert Herrick, who can range from the bawdy to the devotional in a way not to be guessed from the few poems he is usually represented by. It was also good to be able to give less well-known or half-known poets a little more leg-room: people like Drummond and Quarles, and, later, Andrew Young.

One unexpected side-effect of this length limitation is that it throws into relief the gradual change of tone from one generation to the next; in a selection like this you can move through the productions of fifty or sixty years in a few pages and yet read enough of them for the slow shift to be heard. The vernacular unembarrassed directness of the earliest lyrics drifts naturally into the courtly simplicity (which is still robust) of Sir Thomas Wyatt. Courtliness in turn becomes refinement (learnt from Italy), then over-refinement (ordinary life seems to disappear), and this, filtering slightly down the social scale, becomes the urban-genteel of the eighteenth century (even the rural poems are urbane) which arrives at a virtual standstill. Most selections of poems published in the eighteenth century were almost insufferably dull. It is obvious something has to happen, and William Blake arrives, breaks the tight grip of Reason and reasonableness and sounds, at last, like a poet who has no wish to appear a gentleman. He clears the way for the nineteenth century and makes possible the return of two kinds of naturalness, that of Clare and that of Byron. The nineteenth century, in a sense, relaxes. It may seem odd to suggest that brevity can be a form of expansiveness, but so it seems to be; it is a return of confidence in poetry itself, the variety of things it can include, and the variety of means of approach it can use. The process is greatly assisted by the early Americans, such as Emerson and Thoreau, who show ease (though not easiness) in advance of their English counterparts; they would not be out of place, in tone, among the Medievals. Confidence in the short poem continues into the twentieth century until we come to the great masters in brevity of any period: Hardy, Yeats, Frost.

If one can detect a similarity of tone and diction and then its slow change, because poets tend to write differently from their predecessors, this is also because, at any given time, they tend to write astonishingly like each other. What has been exciting for us has been to notice how a poet, perhaps only in one poem, can suddenly leap out of his time and into ours, not by being different from his time but by being better. Thomas Bastard, really looking at a child trying to talk, is an example.

There is in this book an historical imbalance. As has been said, we found the eighteenth-century poets not very fruitful for our purposes. We went deeper and deeper into them, emerging with little. This is partly because they tended to write at length or went in for banal songs or self-sealing, rather self-delighted, epigrams. We set our faces against even successful epigrams because there are already collections of these, and they usually belong to the category of verse rather than that of poetry. But we have let a few pass because we could not resist them—such as the one by Pope to be 'engraved on the collar of a dog'—when they seemed to have a resonance that opened them up, rather than clicking tightly shut, like boxes. Even during the eighteenth century we have chosen only poems we found interesting, for whatever reason; we never tried merely to be representative.

How could we be sure, though, that we were not just preferring poems that spoke to the limited prejudices of our time? We could not, nor did it much matter; every anthology is a 'period piece'. But it was both encouraging and chastening to discover, very often, that the poems and poets that jumped out at us had already done so to earlier, far more scholarly sifters and compilers, pioneers in the field: men such as Grosart, Saintsbury, Chambers, Fellowes, Ault (and there are others; in our own time, there is Mr Geoffrey Grigson). When we went back to the original texts, we almost invariably found (though dearly wanting to be pioneers in our own right) that they had been there ahead of us. This was not only reassuring; it was significant in a much more important sense: it suggests that there is a consensus, bridging generations and different types of people, as to what constitutes a poem that works. This is not a fashionable notion, perhaps. But these men, and others, put together for us the canon of English poetry, and did it so well that it was one of the surprise pleasures of compiling this anthology to delve where they had delved and to watch them, as it were, at work. But the great pleasure was the poems themselves, their variety of mood and subject and tone, a variety that was all the more noticeable, and pleasurable (as we had hoped at the outset) because they were short.

We would like to thank the following for their help at various stages of this selection: Kingsley Amis, Jonathan Barker, Geoffrey Grigson, Roger Lonsdale; the staffs of the Bodleian Library,

INTRODUCTION

Oxford, and St Paul's and St Mary's College, Cheltenham; and, above all, for their help throughout, Clare Asquith and Kate Kavanagh.

1985   P.J.K. and J.M.

xl

ANONYMOUS
13th and 14th centuries

1   *'Fowls in the frith'*

Fowls in the frith,
Fishes in the flood,
And I must wax wod:
Much sorrow I walk with
For best of bone and blood.

2   *'Lord, Thou clèpedest me'*

Lord, Thou clèpedest me,
And I naught ne answerèd Thee
But wordès slow and sleepy:
'Thole yet! Thole a little!'
But 'yet' and 'yet' was endèless,
And 'thole a little' a long way is.

3   *'When I see on Rood'*

When I see on Rood
Jesu, my leman,
And beside him stonden
Mary and Johan,
And his rig iswongen,
And his side istungen,
For the love of Man,
Well ought I to wepen
And sins for to leten,
If I of love can,
If I of love can,
If I of love can.

---

1 frith] wood   wax wod] go mad   1.5] because of the best creature living
2 Rood] the Cross   clèpedest] called   thole] wait
3 leman] lover   rig] back   iswongen] scourged   istungen] pierced   leten] abandon
can] know

ANONYMOUS

4   *'Why have you no ruth?'*

Why have you no ruth on my child?
Have ruth on me, full of mourning.
Take down from Rood my dearworthy child,
Or prick me on Rood with my darling.

More pain ne may me be done
Than letten me liven in sorrow and shame.
As love me bindeth to my son,
So let us dyen bothen isame.

GEOFFREY CHAUCER

1340?–1400

5   *Roundel*

from *The Parliament of Fowls*

Now welcome, summer, with thy sunnė soft,
That hast this winter's wedres overshake
And driven away the longė nightės black!

Saint Valentine, that art full high aloft,
Thus singen smallė fowlės for thy sake:
    'Now welcome, summer, with thy sunnė soft,
    That hast this winter's wedres overshake!'

Well have they causė for to gladden oft,
Since each of them recovered hath his make;
Full blissful may they singė when they wake:
    'Now welcome, summer, with thy sunnė soft,
    That hast this winter's wedres overshake
    And driven away the longė nightes black!'

4 ruth] pity   prick] nail   bothen isame] both together
5 wedres] storms   overshake] shaken off   make] mate

6 ## *Unto Adam, His Own Scrivèyn*

Adam scrivèyn, if ever it thee befall
Boece or *Troilus* for to writen new,
Under thy long locks thou must have the scall
But after my making thou write more true!
So oft a-day I must thy work renew,
It to correct and eke to rub and scrape;
And all is through thy negligence and rape.

7 ## *Roundel*

from *Merciless Beauty*

Since I from Love escapèd am so fat,
I never think to be his prisoner lean;
Since I am free, I count him not a bean.

He may answère and sayè this and that;
I do no fors, I speak right as I mean.
    Since I from Love escapèd am so fat,
    I never think to be his prisoner lean.

Love hath my name y-struck out of his slat,
And he is struck out of my bookès clean
For evermore—there is no other mene.
    Since I from Love escapèd am so fat,
    I never think to be his prisoner lean;
    Since I am free, I count him not a bean.

6 scrivèyn] scribe   Boece] Boethius   thou must] you deserve to   scall] scabies
but] unless   renew] revise   eke] also   rape] haste
7 think] intend   I do no fors] I don't care   y-struck out of his slat] struck off his
slate   mene] course

ANONYMOUS

15th and early 16th centuries

8   *'I shall say what inordinate love is'*

I shall say what inordinate love is:
The furiosity and wodness of mind,
An instinguible brenning, fawting bliss,
A great hunger insatiate to find,
A dulcet ill, an evil sweetness blind,
A right wonderful, sugared, sweet error,
Without labour rest, contrary to kind,
Or without quiet to have huge labour.

9   ## 'Omnes gentes plaudite!'

Omnes gentes plaudite!
I saw many birds sitten on a tree;
They tooken their flight and flowen away
With *Ego dixi*, have a good day!
Many white feathers hath the pie—
I may no more singen, my lips are so dry.
Many white feathers hath the swan—
The more that I drink, the less good I can.
Lay sticks on the fire, well may it brenne!
Give us one drink ere we go henne.

---

8 wodness] frenzy   1. 3] an inextinguishable burning lacking happiness   kind] nature
9 title, 1. 1] O clap your hands together, all ye people! (Psalm 47)   *Ego dixi*] I have
spoken   pie] magpie   good I can] sense I have   brenne] burn   henne] hence

10
'Blessed Mary'

Blessed Mary, mother virginal,
Integrate maiden, star of the sea,
Have remembrance at the day final
On thy poor servant now praying to thee.
Mirror without spot, red rose of Jericho,
Close garden of grace, hope in disparàge,
When my soul the body partè fro,
Succour it from mine enemies' rage.

11
'Peace maketh plenty'

Peace maketh plenty;
Plenty maketh pride;
Pride maketh plea;
Plea maketh povert;
Povert maketh peace.

12
'Hail, Queen of Heaven'

Hail, Queen of Heaven and star of bliss!
Since that thy son thy father is,
How should He any thing thee warn,
And thou His mother and He thy bairn?

Hail, fresh fountain that springès new,
The root and crop of all virtue,
Thou polished gem without offence—
Thou bare the Lamb of Innocence.

10 integrate] perfect   close] enclosed   disparàge] despair   partè fro] departs from
11 plea] lawsuit
12 warn] deny

ANONYMOUS

13   *'I have been a foster'*

I have been a foster long and many day;
    My lockès be hoar.
I shall hang up my horn by the greenwood spray;
    Foster will I be no more.

All the while that I may my bow bend
    Shall I weddè no wife.
I shall bigge me a bower at the woodè's end,
    There to lead my life.

14   *'Western wind'*

Western wind, when will thou blow,
The small rain down can rain?
Christ, if my love were in my arms,
And I in my bed again!

JOHN SKELTON
1460?–1529

15   *'Though ye suppose'*

Though ye suppose all jeopardies are past,
    And all is done ye lookèd for before,
Ware yet, I rede you, of Fortune's double cast,
    For one false point she is wont to keep in store,
    And under the fell oft festered is the sore:
That when ye think all danger for to pass
Ware of the lizard lieth lurking in the grass.

13 foster] forester   bigge] build
14 the] so that the
15 rede] advise   fell] skin

6

SIR THOMAS WYATT

1503–1542

16   *'Madam, withouten many words'*

Madam, withouten many words,
Once, I am sure, ye will or no:
And if ye will, then leave your bourds,
And use your wit, and show it so.

And with a beck ye shall me call,
And if of one that burneth alway
Ye have any pity at all,
Answer him fair with yea or nay.

If it be yea, I shall be fain;
If it be nay, friends as before:
Ye shall another man obtain,
And I mine own, and yours no more.

17   *'Who hath heard'*

Who hath heard of such cruelty before?
That when my plaint remembered her my woe
That caused it, she cruel more and more
Wished each stitch as she did sit and sew
Had pricked mine heart, for to increase my sore.
And, as I think, she thought it had been so:
For as she thought, 'This is his heart indeed',
She pricked hard, and made herself to bleed.

16 bourds] teasing   beck] nod

7

18 *'The enemy of life'*

The enemy of life, decayer of all kind,
That with his cold withers away the green,
This other night me in my bed did find,
And offered me to rid my fever clean;
And I did grant, so did despair me blind.
He drew his bow with arrow sharp and keen,
And struck the place where love had hit before,
And drove the first dart deeper more and more.

19 *'Sighs are my food'*

Sighs are my food, drink are my tears,
Clinking of fetters such music would crave;
Stink and close air away my life wears,
Innocency is all the hope I have;
Rain, wind, or weather I judge by mine ears;
Malice assaulted that righteousness should have.
Sure I am, Brian, this wound shall heal again,
But yet, alas, the scar shall still remain.

20 *'Lux, my fair falcon'*

Lux, my fair falcon, and your fellows all,
How well pleasant it were your liberty!
Ye not forsake me that fair might ye befall,
But they that sometime liked my company,
Like lice away from dead bodies they crawl.
Lo, what a proof in light adversity!
But ye, my birds, I swear by all your bells
Ye be my friends, and so be but few else.

19 that] that which

8

SIR THOMAS WYATT

'Throughout the world'

21

Throughout the world if it were sought,
  Fair words enough a man shall find;
They be good cheap, they cost right nought,
  Their substance is but only wind.
But well to say and so to mean,
That sweet accord is seldom seen.

WILLIAM BALDWIN

c.1515–1563

The Spouse to the Younglings

22

Christ my Beloved which still doth feed
  Among the flowers, having delight
    Among his faithful lilies,

Doth take great care for me indeed,
  And I again with all my might
    Will do what so his will is.

My Love in me, and I in him,
  Conjoined by love will still abide
    Among the faithful lilies

Till day do break, and truth do dim
  All shadows dark, and cause them slide
    According as his will is.

22 title] The Bride to the Maidens   still] forever

ANONYMOUS

c.1550

23   *'Thou sleepest fast'*

Thou sleepest fast, and I with woeful heart
    Stand here alone sighing and cannot fly:
Thou sleepest fast, when cruel Love his dart
    On me doth cast, alas, so painfully!
Thou sleepest fast, and I, all full of smart,
    To thee, my foe, in vain do call and cry:
And yet, methinkes, though thou sleepest fast
Thou dreamest still which way my life to waste.

GEORGE TURBERVILE

1540?–1610

24 *To an Old Gentlewoman that Painted Her Face*

Leave off, good Beroë, now
To sleek thy shrivelled skin,
For Hecube's face will never be
As Helen's hue hath been.

Let beauty go with youth,
Renounce the glozing glass,
Take Book in hand: that seemly rose
Is woxen withered grass.

Remove thy peacock's plumes,
Thou crank and curious dame;
To other trulls of tender years
Resign the flag of fame.

24 glozing] flattering   woxen] become   crank and curious] conceited and fussy
trulls] wenches

SIR EDWARD DYER

*c.*1545–1607

25   *'The lowest trees have tops'*

The lowest trees have tops, the ant her gall,
   The fly her spleen, the little spark his heat;
The slender hairs cast shadows, though but small,
   And bees have stings, although they be not great;
Seas have their source, and so have shallow springs;
And love is love, in beggars and in kings.

Where rivers smoothest run, there deepest are the fords;
   The dial stirs, yet none perceives it move;
The firmest faith is in the fewest words;
   The turtles cannot sing, and yet they love;
True hearts have eyes and ears, no tongues to speak:
They hear and see, and sigh, and then they break.

EDWARD DE VERE, EARL OF OXFORD

1550–1604

26   *Epigram*

Were I a king, I might command content,
   Were I obscure, unknown should be my cares,
And were I dead, no thoughts should me torment,
   Nor words, nor wrongs, nor loves, nor hate, nor fears.
A doubtful choice for me, of three things one to crave:
A kingdom, or a cottage, or a grave.

25 turtles] turtle doves

SIR WALTER RALEGH
1552?–1618

27   *To His Son*

Three things there be that prosper all apace,
  And flourish while they are asunder far;
But on a day they meet all in a place,
  And when they meet they one another mar.

And they be these—the wood, the weed, the wag:
  The wood is that that makes the gallows tree;
The weed is that that strings the hangman's bag;
  The wag, my pretty knave, betokens thee.

Now mark, dear boy, while these assemble not,
  Green springs the tree, hemp grows, the wag is wild;
But when they meet, it makes the timber rot,
  It frets the halter, and it chokes the child.
  God bless the child.

28   *'What is our life?'*

What is our life? A play of passion;
Our mirth the music of division;
Our mothers' wombs the tiring-houses be
Where we are dressed for this short comedy;
Heaven the judicious sharp spectator is
That sits and marks still who doth act amiss;
Our graves that hide us from the searching sun
Are like drawn curtains when the play is done.
Thus march we playing to our latest rest,
Only we die in earnest, that's no jest.

28 division] variations   tiring-houses] dressing rooms

SIR WALTER RALEGH

29 *'Even such is time'*

Even such is time, which takes in trust
Our youth, our joys, and all we have,
And pays us but with age and dust:
Who in the dark and silent grave
When we have wandered all our ways
Shuts up the story of our days.
And from which earth and grave and dust
The Lord shall raise me up, I trust.

SIR PHILIP SIDNEY
1554–1586

30 *'Sleep, baby mine, Desire'*

'Sleep, baby mine, Desire,' nurse Beauty singeth,
'Thy cries, O baby, set mine head on aching.'
The babe cries, ''Way, thy love doth keep me waking.'

'Lully, lully, my babe; Hope cradle bringeth
Unto my children, always good rest taking.'
The babe cries, ''Way, thy love doth keep me waking.'

'Since, baby mine, from me thy watching springeth,
Sleep then a little, pap content is making.'
The babe cries, 'Nay, for that abide I waking.'

30 pap] breast milk

13

31   *'Like those sick folks'*

Like those sick folks in whom strange humours flow
Can taste no sweets, the sour only please,
So to my mind, while passions daily grow,
Whose fiery chains upon his freedom seize,
Joys strangers seem, I cannot bide their show,
Nor brook aught else but well-acquainted woe.
Bitter grief tastes me best, pain is my ease,
Sick to the death, still loving my disease.

FULKE GREVILLE, LORD BROOKE

1554–1628

32   *'Whenas man's life'*

Whenas man's life, the light of human lust,
In socket of his earthly lantern burns,
That all this glory unto ashes must,
And generation to corruption turns;
    Then fond desires that only fear their end
    Do vainly wish for life, but to amend.

But when this life is from the body fled,
To see itself in that eternal glass
Where time doth end and thoughts accuse the dead,
Where all to come is one with all that was;
    Then living men ask how he left his breath
    That while he livèd never thought of death.

GEORGE PEELE
1558?–1597

33

Bethsabe's Song

from *David and Bethsabe*

Hot sun, cool fire, tempered with sweet air,
Black shade, fair nurse, shadow my white hair,
Shine, sun, burn, fire, breathe, air, and ease me,
Black shade, fair nurse, shroud me and please me;
Shadow, my sweet nurse, keep me from burning,
Make not my glad cause, cause of mourning.
    Let not my beauty's fire
    Inflame unstaid desire,
    Nor pierce any bright eye
    That wandereth lightly.

GEORGE CHAPMAN
1559?–1634

34

Bridal Song

from *The Masque of the Middle Temple and Lincoln's Inn*

Now, Sleep, bind fast the flood of air,
    Strike all things dumb and deaf,
And to disturb our nuptial pair
    Let stir no aspen leaf.
Send flocks of golden dreams
    That all true joys presage;
Bring, in thy oily streams,
    The milk-and-honey age.
Now close the world-round sphere of bliss,
And fill it with a heavenly kiss.

15

ANONYMOUS
printed 1599–1610

35   *'Thyrsis, sleepest thou?'*

'Thyrsis, sleepest thou? Holla! Let not sorrow slay us.
Hold up thy head, man,' said the gentle Meliboeus.
'See, summer comes again, the country's pride adorning.
Hark how the cuckoo singeth this fair April morning.'
'O,' said the shepherd, and sighed as one all undone,
'Let me alone, alas, and drive him back to London.'

36   *'A sparrow-hawk proud'*

A sparrow-hawk proud did hold in wicked jail
Music's sweet chorister, the nightingale;
To whom with sighs she said, 'O set me free,
And in my song I'll praise no bird but thee.'
The hawk replied, 'I will not lose my diet
To let a thousand such enjoy their quiet.'

37   *Thule*

Thule, the period of cosmography,
   Doth vaunt of Hecla, whose sulphureous fire
Doth melt the frozen clime and thaw the sky;
   Trinacrian Etna's flames ascend not higher.
These things seem wondrous, yet more wondrous I,
Whose heart with fear doth freeze, with love doth fry.

The Andalusian merchant, that returns
   Laden with cochineal and China dishes,
Reports in Spain how strangely Fogo burns
   Amidst an ocean full of flying fishes.
These things seem wondrous, yet more wondrous I,
Whose heart with fear doth freeze, with love doth fry.

37 period] limit

16

38 *'My love in her attire'*

My love in her attire doth show her wit,
  It doth so well become her:
For every season she hath dressings fit,
  For winter, spring, and summer.
No beauty she doth miss
  When all her robes are on;
But Beauty's self she is
  When all her robes are gone.

39 *'Since first I saw your face'*

Since first I saw your face, I resolved to honour and renown ye;
If now I be disdained, I wish my heart had never known ye.
What? I that loved and you that liked, shall we begin to
    wrangle?
No, no, no, my heart is fast, and cannot disentangle.

If I admire or praise you too much, that fault you may forgive
    me;
Or if my hands had strayed but a touch, then justly might you
    leave me.
I asked you leave, you bade me love; is't now a time to chide
    me?
No, no, no, I'll love you still what fortune e'er betide me.

The sun, whose beams most glorious are, rejecteth no beholder,
And your sweet beauty past compare made my poor eyes the
    bolder;
Where beauty moves and wit delights and signs of kindness
    bind me,
There, O there, where'er I go I'll leave my heart behind me!

ANONYMOUS

40   *'Love me not'*

Love me not for comely grace,
For my pleasing eye or face,
Nor for any outward part,
No, nor for my constant heart;
For those may fail or turn to ill,
    So thou and I shall sever.
Keep therefore a true woman's eye,
And love me still, but know not why,
So hast thou the same reason still
    To dote upon me ever.

41   *'Sweet, let me go!'*

Sweet, let me go! Sweet, let me go!
What do you mean to vex me so?
Cease, cease, cease your pleading force.
Do you think thus to extort remorse?
Now no more; alas, you overbear me;
And I would cry, but some would hear, I fear me.

42   *'He that hath no mistress'*

He that hath no mistress must not wear a favour.
He that woos a mistress must serve before he have her.
He that hath no bed-fellow must lie alone,
And he that hath no lady must be content with Joan.
And so must I, for why? Alas, my love and I are parted.
False Cupid, I will have thee whipped, and have thy mother
    carted.

42 carted] carried by cart through the streets as a punishment

18

43 ### *'Sweet Cupid, ripen her desire'*

Sweet Cupid, ripen her desire,
   Thy joyful harvest may begin;
If age approach a little nigher,
   'Twill be too late to get it in.

Cold winter storms lay standing corn,
   Which once too ripe will never rise,
And lovers wish themselves unborn,
   When all their joys lie in their eyes.

Then, sweet, let us embrace and kiss.
   Shall beauty shale upon the ground?
If age bereave us of this bliss,
   Then will no more such sport be found.

SIR JOHN HARINGTON
1561–1612

44 ### *To His Wife, for Striking Her Dog*

Your little dog that barked as I came by,
I strake by hap so hard I made him cry;
And straight you put your finger in your eye,
And louring sat. I asked the reason why.
'Love me, and love my dog,' thou didst reply,
'Love as both should be loved.' 'I will,' said I,
And sealed it with a kiss. Then, by and by,
Cleared were the clouds of thy fair frowning sky.
Thus small events great masteries may try:
   For I, by this, do at their meaning guess
   That beat a whelp afore a lioness.

43 shale] drop like a husk
44 strake] struck   louring] glowering   masteries] conclusions   try] test

WILLIAM SHAKESPEARE
1564–1616

45   *Song*

from *Twelfth Night*

O mistress mine, where are you roaming?
O stay and hear, your true love's coming
   That can sing both high and low.
Trip no further, pretty sweeting;
Journeys end in lovers meeting,
   Every wise man's son doth know.

What is love? 'Tis not hereafter:
Present mirth hath present laughter,
   What's to come is still unsure.
In delay there lies no plenty,
Then come kiss me, sweet and twenty;
   Youth's a stuff will not endure.

46   *Song*

from *The Winter's Tale*

When daffodils begin to peer,
   With hey, the doxy over the dale!
Why, then comes in the sweet o' the year,
   For the red blood reigns in the winter's pale.

The white sheet bleaching on the hedge,
   With hey, the sweet birds, O how they sing!
Doth set my pugging tooth an edge,
   For a quart of ale is a dish for a king.

45 still] always
46 doxy] wench   1. 7] whets my thieving taste

20

The lark that tirra-lirra chants,
  With hey, with hey! the thrush and the jay
Are summer songs for me and my aunts
  While we lie tumbling in the hay.

47   *Song*

from *The Winter's Tale*

Jog on, jog on, the footpath way,
  And merrily hent the stile-a;
A merry heart goes all the day,
  Your sad tires in a mile-a.

48   *Song*

from *The Tempest*

Full fathom five thy father lies,
  Of his bones are coral made,
Those are pearls that were his eyes:
  Nothing of him that doth fade
But doth suffer a sea-change
Into something rich and strange.
Sea-nymphs hourly ring his knell.
Hark! now I hear them: ding, dong, bell.

46 aunts] girls
47 hent] catch hold of

WILLIAM SHAKESPEARE

49   *Song*
                 from *The Tempest*

The master, the swabber, the boatswain and I,
    The gunner and his mate,
Loved Mall, Meg, and Marian, and Margery,
    But none of us cared for Kate.
    For she had a tongue with a tang,
    Would cry to a sailor, 'Go hang!'
She loved not the savour of tar nor of pitch,
Yet a tailor might scratch her where'er she did itch.
    Then to sea, boys, and let her go hang.

50   *Song*
                 from *The Tempest*

Where the bee sucks, there suck I,
    In a cowslip's bell I lie,
    There I couch when owls do cry,
    On the bat's back I do fly
    After summer merrily.
Merrily, merrily, shall I live now
Under the blossom that hangs on the bough.

JOHN DAVIES OF HEREFORD
1565–1618

51
A Remembrance of My Friend Mr Thomas Morley

Death hath deprived me of my dearest friend;
    My dearest friend is dead and laid in grave.
In grave he rests until the world shall end.
    The world shall end, as end all things must have.
All things must have an end that Nature wrought:
That Nature wrought must unto dust be brought.

22

ROBERT DEVEREUX, EARL OF ESSEX
1566–1601

52   *'Happy were he'*

Happy were he could finish forth his fate
   In some unhaunted desert, most obscure
From all societies, from love and hate
   Of worldly folk; then might he sleep secure;
Then wake again, and give God ever praise,
   Content with hips and haws and bramble-berry;
In contemplation spending all his days,
   And change of holy thoughts to make him merry;
Where, when he dies, his tomb may be a bush,
Where harmless robin dwells with gentle thrush.

THOMAS BASTARD
1566–1618

53   De Puero Balbutiente

Methinks 'tis pretty sport to hear a child
Rocking a word in mouth yet undefiled;
The tender racquet rudely plays the sound
Which, weakly bandied, cannot back rebound;
And the soft air the softer roof doth kiss
With a sweet dying and a pretty miss,
Which hears no answer yet from the white rank
Of teeth not risen from their coral bank.
The alphabet is searched for letters soft
To try a word before it can be wrought;
And when it slideth forth, it goes as nice
As when a man doth walk upon the ice.

53 title] On a Child Learning to Talk   nice] carefully

THOMAS NASHE

1567–1601

54   *'Fair summer droops'*

Fair summer droops, droop men and beasts therefore,
So fair a summer look for never more!
All good things vanish less than in a day,
Peace, plenty, pleasure, suddenly decay.
  Go not yet away, bright soul of the sad year,
  The earth is hell when thou leav'st to appear.

What, shall those flowers that decked thy garland erst
Upon thy grave be wastefully dispersed?
O trees, consume your sap in sorrow's source,
Streams, turn to tears your tributary course.
  Go not yet hence, bright soul of the sad year,
  The earth is hell when thou leav'st to appear.

THOMAS CAMPION

1567–1620

55   *'When thou must home'*

When thou must home to shades of underground,
And there arrived, a new admirèd guest,
The beauteous spirits do engirt thee round,
White Iope, blithe Helen, and the rest,
To hear the stories of thy finished love
From that smooth tongue whose music Hell can move,

54 leav'st] ceasest

Then wilt thou speak of banqueting delights,
Of masques and revels which sweet youth did make,
Of tourneys and great challenges of knights,
And all these triumphs for thy beauty's sake.
When thou hast told these honours done to thee,
Then tell, O tell, how thou didst murder me.

56   *'Never weather-beaten sail'*

Never weather-beaten sail more willing bent to shore,
Never tired pilgrim's limbs affected slumber more
Than my weary sprite now longs to fly out of my troubled
    breast.
O come quickly, sweetest Lord, and take my soul to rest.

Ever-blooming are the joys of Heaven's high paradise,
Cold age deafs not there our ears, nor vapour dims our eyes,
Glory there the sun outshines, whose beams the blessèd only
    see.
O come quickly, glorious Lord, and raise my sprite to thee.

57   *'Thrice toss these oaken ashes in the air'*

Thrice toss these oaken ashes in the air,
Thrice sit thou mute in this enchanted chair,
And thrice three times tie up this true love's knot,
And murmur soft, 'She will, or she will not.'

Go burn these poisonous weeds in yon blue fire,
These screech-owl's feathers and this prickling briar,
This cypress gathered at a dead man's grave,
That all thy fears and cares an end may have.

Then come, you fairies, dance with me a round!
Melt her hard heart with your melodious sound!
In vain are all the charms I can devise:
She hath an art to break them with her eyes.

56 affected] sought

25

58 *'Thus I resolve'*

Thus I resolve, and time hath taught me so:
Since she is fair and ever kind to me,
Though she be wild and wanton-like in show,
Those little stains in youth I will not see.
    That she be constant Heaven I oft implore;
    If prayers prevail not, I can do no more.

Palm tree the more you press, the more it grows;
Leave it alone, it will not much exceed.
Free beauty if you strive to yoke, you lose,
And for affection strange distaste you breed.
    What Nature hath not taught, no art can frame:
    Wild born be wild still, though by force made tame.

59 *'Sleep, angry beauty'*

Sleep, angry beauty, sleep, and fear not me.
For who a sleeping lion dares provoke?
It shall suffice me here to sit and see
Those lips shut up that never kindly spoke.
    What sight can more content a lover's mind
    Than beauty seeming harmless, if not kind?

My words have charmed her, for secure she sleeps,
Though guilty of much wrong done to my love;
And in her slumber, see, she close-eyed weeps:
Dreams often more than waking passions move.
    Plead, sleep, my cause, and make her soft like thee,
    That she in peace may wake and pity me.

60 *'Think'st thou to seduce me then'*

Think'st thou to seduce me then with words that have no
    meaning?
Parrots so can learn to prate, our speech by pieces gleaning,
Nurses teach their children so, about the time of weaning.

Learn to speak first, then to woo: to wooing much pertaineth.
He that courts us, wanting art, soon falters when he feigneth,
Looks asquint on his discourse and smiles when he complaineth.

Skilful anglers hide their hooks, fit baits for every season,
But with crooked pins fish thou, as babes do that want reason:
Gudgeons only can be caught with such poor tricks of treason.

Ruth forgive me if I erred from human heart's compassion,
When I laughed sometimes too much to see thy foolish fashion.
But, alas, who less could do that found so good occasion?

THOMAS MIDDLETON
1570?–1627

61   *Song*

from *The Witch*

In a maiden-time professed,
Then we say that life is best;
Tasting once the married life,
Then we only praise the wife;
There's but one state more to try
Which makes women laugh or cry—
Widow, widow. Of these three
The middle's best, and that give me.

**60 ruth] pity

27

SAMUEL ROWLANDS
1570?–1630?

62   *Melancholy Conceit*

Rapier, lie there! and there, my hat and feather!
   Draw my silk curtain to obscure the light,
Goose-quill and I must join awhile together:
   Lady, forbear, I pray, keep out of sight!
Call Pearl away, let one remove him hence!
Your shrieking parrot will distract my sense.

Would I were near the rogue that crieth, 'Black!'
   'Buy a new almanac!' doth vex me too:
Forbid the maid she wind not up the jack!
   Take hence my watch, it makes too much ado!
Let none come at me, dearest friend or kin:
Whoe'er it be I am not now within.

BEN JONSON
1572–1637

63   *Song*

from *Cynthia's Revels*

Slow, slow, fresh fount, keep time with my salt tears;
   Yet slower, yet, O faintly, gentle springs;
List to the heavy part the music bears,
   Woe weeps out her division when she sings.
      Droop herbs and flowers,
      Fall grief in showers,
      Our beauties are not ours.
         O, I could still,
Like melting snow upon some craggy hill,
      Drop, drop, drop, drop,
Since Nature's pride is now a withered daffodil.

---

62 'Black'] street cry (blacking polish)   jack] figure striking the bell on a clock
63 division] musical variations

BEN JONSON

64   *On My First Son*

Farewell, thou child of my right hand, and joy;
My sin was too much hope of thee, loved boy.
Seven years thou wert lent to me, and I thee pay,
Exacted by thy fate, on the just day.
O, could I lose all father now! For why
Will man lament the state he should envỳ?
To have so soon 'scaped world's and flesh's rage,
And, if no other misery, yet age!
Rest in soft peace, and, asked, say here doth lie
Ben Jonson his best piece of poetry;
For whose sake, henceforth, all his vows be such
As what he loves may never like too much.

65   *Song*

from *The Silent Woman*

Still to be neat, still to be dressed
As you were going to a feast;
Still to be powdered, still perfumed:
Lady, it is to be presumed,
Though art's hid causes are not found,
All is not sweet, all is not sound.
Give me a look, give me a face,
That makes simplicity a grace;
Robes loosely flowing, hair as free:
Such sweet neglect more taketh me
Than all the adulteries of art;
They strike mine eyes, but not my heart.

66 *Why I Write Not of Love*

Some act of Love's bound to rehearse,
I thought to bind him in my verse;
Which when he felt, 'Away,' quoth he,
'Can poets hope to fetter me?
It is enough they once did get
Mars and my mother in their net:
I wear not these my wings in vain.'
With which he fled me, and again
Into my rhymes could ne'er be got
By any art. Then wonder not
That since, my numbers are so cold,
When Love is fled and I grow old.

67 *On Something that Walks Somewhere*

At court I met it, in clothes brave enough
To be a courtier, and looks grave enough
To seem a statesman. As I near it came,
It made me a great face. I asked the name.
'A lord,' it cried, 'buried in flesh and blood,
And such from whom let no man hope least good,
For I will do none; and as little ill,
For I will dare none.' Good lord, walk dead still.

68 *On Spies*

Spies, you are lights in state, but of base stuff,
Who, when you've burnt yourselves down to the snuff,
Stink, and are thrown away. End fair enough.

69 *To Fine Lady Would-Be*

Fine Madam Would-be, wherefore should you fear,
That love to make so well, a child to bear?
The world reputes you barren; but I know
Your 'pothecary and his drug says no.
Is it the pain affrights? That's soon forgot.
Or your complexion's loss? You have a pot
That can restore that. Will it hurt your feature?
To make amends, you're thought a wholesome creature.
What should the cause be? Oh, you live at court:
And there's both loss of time and loss of sport
In a great belly. Write then on thy womb:
Of the not born, yet buried, here's the tomb.

70 *Song: That Women are but Men's Shadows*

Follow a shadow, it still flies you;
Seem to fly it, it will pursue:
So court a mistress, she denies you;
Let her alone, she will court you.
Say, are not women truly then
Styled but the shadows of us men?
At morn and even shades are longest;
At noon they are or short or none:
So men at weakest, they are strongest,
But grant us perfect, they're not known.
Say, are not women truly then
Styled but the shadows of us men?

69 make] make love

31

71 *A Fragment of Petronius*

Doing, a filthy pleasure is, and short;
And done, we straight repent us of the sport.
Let us not then rush blindly on unto it,
Like lustful beasts that only know to do it,
For lust will languish, and that heat decay,
But thus, thus, keeping endless holiday,
Let us together closely lie, and kiss,
There is no labour, nor no shame in this;
This hath pleased, doth please, and long will please; never
Can this decay, but is beginning ever.

72 *Song*

from *The Gypsies Metamorphosed*

The fairy beam upon you,
The stars to glister on you:
   A moon of light,
   In the noon of night,
Till the fire-drake hath o'ergone you.

The wheel of fortune guide you,
The boy with the bow beside you
   Run aye in the way
   Till the bird of day,
And the luckier lot betide you.

72 Fire-drake] meteor

73
Song
from *The Gypsies Metamorphosed*

To the old, long life and treasure;
To the young, all health and pleasure;
    To the fair, their face
    With eternal grace,
And the soul to be loved at leisure.
To the witty, all clear mirrors;
To the foolish, their dark errors;
To the loving sprite,
A secure delight;
To the jealous, his own false terrors.

74
'Here she was wont to go'
from *The Sad Shepherd*

Here she was wont to go, and here, and here!
Just where those daisies, pinks, and violets grow.
The world may find the spring by following her,
For other print her airy steps ne'er left:
Her treading would not bend a blade of grass,
Or shake the downy blow-ball from his stalk;
But like the soft west wind she shot along,
And where she went the flowers took thickest root,
As she had sowed them with her odorous foot.

74 blow-ball] dandelion-head

JOHN DONNE
1573–1631

75
The Computation

For the first twenty years, since yesterday,
I scarce believed thou couldst be gone away;
For forty more, I fed on favours past,
And forty on hopes—that thou wouldst, they might, last.
Tears drowned one hundred, and sighs blew out two;
A thousand, I did neither think, nor do,
Or not divide, all being one thought of you;
Or in a thousand more forgot that too.
Yet call not this long life, but think that I
Am, by being dead, immortal. Can ghosts die?

76
The Expiration

So, so, break off this last lamenting kiss,
    Which sucks two souls, and vapours both, away;
Turn thou, ghost, that way, and let me turn this,
    And let our selves benight our happiest day.
We asked none leave to love, nor will we owe
Any so cheap a death as saying, Go.

Go; and if that word have not quite killed thee,
    Ease me with death by bidding me go too.
Oh, if it have, let my word work on me,
    And a just office on a murderer do.
Except it be too late to kill me so,
Being double dead: going, and bidding go.

A Jet Ring Sent

77

Thou art not so black as my heart,
 Nor half so brittle as her heart thou art;
What wouldst thou say? shall both our properties by thee be
  spoke:
Nothing more endless, nothing sooner broke?

Marriage rings are not of this stuff;
 Oh, why should aught less precious or less tough
Figure our loves? Except in thy name thou have bid it say,
 I am cheap, and nought but fashion: fling me away.

Yet stay with me since thou art come:
 Circle this finger's top, which didst her thumb.
Be justly proud, and gladly safe, that thou dost dwell with me:
 She that, oh, broke her faith, would soon break thee.

RICHARD BARNFIELD

1574–1627

78   *A Comparison of the Life of Man*

Man's life is well comparèd to a feast,
 Furnished with choice of all variety;
To it comes Time, and as a bidden guest
 He sets him down in pomp and majesty;
The threefold age of man the waiters be:
 Then with an earthen voider, made of clay,
Comes Death, and takes the table clean away.

78 voider] plate for scraps

THOMAS BEEDOME

?–1641

79   *To the Noble Sir Francis Drake*

Drake, who the world hast conquered like a scroll,
Who saw'st the Arctic and Antarctic Pole,
If men were silent, stars would make thee known:
Phoebus forgets not his companion.

THOMAS HEYWOOD

1574?–1641

80   *An Epitaph*

I was, I am not; smiled, that since did weep;
Laboured, that rest; I waked, that now must sleep;
I played, I play not; sung, that now am still;
Saw, that am blind; I would, that have no will;
I fed that which feeds worms; I stood, I fell;
I bade God save you, that now bid farewell;
I felt, I feel not; followed, was pursued;
I warred, have peace; I conquered, am subdued;
I moved, want motion; I was stiff, that bow
Below the earth; then something, nothing now;
I catched, am caught; I travelled, here I lie;
Lived in the world, that to the world now die.

JOHN FLETCHER
1579–1625

81

The River-God's Song

from *The Faithful Shepherdess*

Do not fear to put thy feet
Naked in the river sweet;
Think not leech or newt or toad
Will bite thy foot when thou hast trod;
Nor let the water rising high
As thou wad'st in make thee cry
And sob, but ever live with me,
And not a wave shall trouble thee.

82

Song

from *The Tragedy of Valentinian*

Care-charming Sleep, thou easer of all woes,
Brother to Death, sweetly thyself dispose
On this afflicted prince, fall like a cloud
In gentle showers; give nothing that is loud
Or painful to his slumbers; easy, sweet,
And as a purling stream, thou son of Night,
Pass by his troubled senses; sing his pain
Like hollow murmuring wind, or silver rain;
Into this prince gently, oh gently slide,
And kiss him into slumbers like a bride.

JOHN FLETCHER with FRANCIS BEAUMONT

1584–1616

83
Song

from *The Maid's Tragedy*

Hold back thy hours, dark night, till we have done:
  The day will come too soon.
Young maids will curse thee if thou steal'st away
And leav'st their losses open to the day.
  Stay, stay, and hide
  The blushes of the bride.

Stay, gentle night, and with thy darkness cover
  The kisses of her lover.
Stay, and confound her tears and her shrill cryings,
Her weak denials, vows, and often-dyings;
  Stay, and hide all:
  But help not, though she call.

JOHN DIGBY, EARL OF BRISTOL

1580–1655

84
'Grieve not, dear love'

Grieve not, dear love, although we often part,
But know that Nature gently doth us sever,
Thereby to train us up, with tender art,
To brook the day when we must part for ever.

For Nature, doubting we should be surprised
By that sad day whose dread doth chiefly fear us,
Doth keep us daily schooled and exercised
Lest that the fright thereof should overbear us.

38

DUDLEY, LORD NORTH
1581–1666

85   *Air*

So full of courtly reverence,
    So full of formal fair respect,
Carries a pretty double sense
    Little more pleasing than neglect.

It is not friendly, 'tis not free,
    It holds a distance half unkind;
Such distance between you and me
    May suit with yours, not with my mind.

Oblige me in a more obliging way,
Or know such over-acting spoils the play.

PHINEAS FLETCHER
1582–1659

86   *An Hymn*

Drop, drop, slow tears,
    and bathe those beauteous feet
Which brought from Heaven
    the news and Prince of Peace.
Cease not, wet eyes,
    his mercies to entreat:
To cry for vengeance
    sin doth never cease;
In your deep floods
    drown all my faults and fears,
Nor let His eye
    see sin, but through my tears.

JOHN AMNER

fl. 1615

87   *A Motet*

A stranger here, as all my fathers were
That went before, I wander to and fro;
From earth to heaven is my pilgrimage,
A tedious way for flesh and blood to go.
O Thou that art the way, pity the blind,
And teach me how I may Thy dwelling find.

EDWARD, LORD HERBERT OF CHERBURY

1583–1648

88   *'Inconstancy's the greatest of sins'*

Inconstancy's the greatest of sins:
It neither ends well, nor begins.
All other faults we simply do;
This, 'tis the same fault, and next too.

Inconstancy no sin will prove
If we consider that we love
But the same beauty in another face,
Like the same body in another place.

89   *In a Glass Window, for Inconstancy*

Love, of this clearest, frailest glass
Divide the properties, so as
In the division may appear
Clearness for me, frailty for her.

WILLIAM DRUMMOND OF HAWTHORNDEN
1585–1649

90   *Madrigal*

My thoughts hold mortal strife;
I do detest my life,
And with lamenting cries,
Peace to my soul to bring,
Oft call that prince which here doth monarchise:
But he, grim-grinning king,
Who caitiffs scorns and doth the blest surprise,
Late having decked with beauty's rose his tomb,
Disdains to crop a weed, and will not come.

91   *To Chloris*

See, Chloris, how the clouds
Tilt in the azure lists,
And how with Stygian mists
Each hornèd hill his giant forehead shrouds;
Jove thundereth in the air,
The air grown great with rain
Now seems to bring Deucalion's days again.
I see thee quake: come, let us home repair;
Come, hide thee in mine arms,
If not for love, yet to shun greater harms.

91 Deucalion's days] the Flood in Greek mythology

92 *Madrigal*

This world a hunting is:
The prey poor Man, the Nimrod fierce is Death;
His speedy greyhounds are
Lust, Sickness, Envy, Care,
Strife that ne'er falls amiss,
With all those ills which haunt us while we breathe.
Now if, by chance, we fly
Of these the eager chase,
Old Age with stealing pace
Casts up his nets, and there we panting die.

JOHN FORD

1586?–1639?

93 *Song*

from *The Broken Heart*

Oh, no more, no more. Too late
  Sighs are spent. The burning tapers
Of a life as chaste as fate,
  Pure as are unwritten papers,
Are burnt out. No heat, no light
Now remains. 'Tis ever night.
  Love is dead. Let lovers' eyes,
    Locked in endless dreams,
    Th' extremes of all extremes,
  Ope no more; for now Love dies,
Now Love dies, implying
Love's martyrs must be ever, ever dying.

ANONYMOUS
printed 1611–1651

94   *'Let not the sluggish sleep'*

Let not the sluggish sleep
   Close up thy waking eye,
Until with judgment deep
   Thy daily deeds thou try.

He that one sin in conscience keeps
   When he to quiet goes,
More venturous is than he that sleeps
   With twenty mortal foes.

95   *'The silver swan'*

The silver swan, who living had no note,
When death approached, unlocked her silent throat,
Leaning her breast against the reedy shore,
Thus sung her first and last, and sung no more:
'Farewell all joys! O death, come close mine eyes;
More geese than swans now live, more fools than wise.'

96   *'Love is a secret feeding fire'*

Love is a secret feeding fire that gives all creatures being,
Life to the dead, speech to the dumb, and to the blind man
   seeing.
And yet in me he contradicts all these his sacred graces:
Sears up my lips, my eyes, my life, and from me ever flying
Leads me in paths untracked, ungone, and many uncouth
   places,
Where in despair I beauty curse. Curse love and all fair faces!

ANONYMOUS

97   *'Art thou that she?'*

'Art thou that she than whom none fairer is,
Art thou that she desire so strives to kiss?'
   'Say I am: how then?
     Maids may not kiss
   Such wanton-humoured men.'

'Art thou that she the world commends for wit?
Art thou so wise and mak'st no use of it?'
   'Say I am: how then?
     My wit doth teach me shun
   Such foolish, foolish men.'

98   *'As life what is so sweet?'*

As life what is so sweet?
What creature would not choose thee?
The wounded hart doth weep
When he is forced to lose thee,
The bruisèd worm doth strive 'gainst fear of death,
And all choose life with pain ere loss of breath.

The dove which knows no guilt
Weeps for her mate a-dying;
And never any blood was spilt
But left the loser crying.
If swans do sing, it is to crave of Death
He would not reave them of their happy breath.

98 reave] rob

44

99

'Three score and ten'

Three score and ten, the life and age of man,
In holy David's eyes seemed but a span;
And half the time is lost and spent in sleep,
So only thirty-five for use we keep.
Our days of youth must be abated all:
Childhood and youth wise Solomon doth call
But vanity. 'Vanity,' he says,
'Is what befalls us in our childish days.'
Our days of age we take no pleasure in;
Our days of grief we wish had never been:
So age deducted, sleep, and youth, and sorrow,
Only one span is all the life we borrow.

100

De Morte

Man's life's a tragedy. His mother's womb,
From which he enters, is the tiring-room;
This spacious earth the theatre, and the stage
That country which he lives in; Passions, Rage,
Folly, and Vice are actors; the first cry
The prologue to th'ensuing tragedy.
The former act consisteth of dumb shows;
The second, he to more perfection grows;
I' the third he is a man, and doth begin
To nurture vice and act the deeds of sin;
I' the fourth declines; i' the fifth diseases clog
And trouble him; then death's his epilogue.

99 abated] excepted
100 title] On Death   tiring-room] dressing-room

ROBERT HERRICK
1591–1674

101   *Discontents in Devon*

More discontents I never had
    Since I was born, than here,
Where I have been, and still am, sad,
    In this dull Devonshire.
Yet justly too I must confess:
    I ne'er invested such
Ennobled numbers for the press
    Than where I loathed so much.

102   *Dreams*

Here we are all, by day; by night we are hurled
By dreams, each one into a several world.

103   *Impossibilities, to His Friend*

My faithful friend, if you can see
The fruit to grow up, or the tree;
If you can see the colour come
Into the blushing pear or plum;
If you can see the water grow
To cakes of ice, or flakes of snow;
If you can see that drop of rain
Lost in the wild sea once again;
If you can see how dreams do creep
Into the brain by easy sleep:
Then there is hope that you may see
Her love me once, who now hates me.

ROBERT HERRICK

104 *Upon Himself*

Mop-eyed I am, as some have said,
Because I've lived so long a maid;
But grant that I should wedded be,
Should I a jot the better see?
No, I should think that marriage might,
Rather than mend, put out the light.

105 *The Coming of Good Luck*

So good luck came, and on my roof did light
Like noiseless snow, or as the dew of night:
Not all at once, but gently, as the trees
Are by the sunbeams tickled by degrees.

106 *The Silken Snake*

For sport my Julia threw a lace
Of silk and silver at my face.
Watchet the silk was, and did make
A show, as if't had been a snake:
The suddenness did me affright,
But though it scared, it did not bite.

107 *To Daisies, Not to Shut So Soon*

Shut not so soon; the dull-eyed night
  Has not as yet begun
To make a seizure on the light,
  Or to seal up the sun.

104 mop-eyed] myopic
106 watchet] sky-blue

47

No marigolds yet closèd are,
    No shadows great appear,
Nor doth the early shepherd's star
    Shine like a spangle here.

Stay but till my Julia close
    Her life-begetting eye;
And let the whole world then dispose
    Itself to live or die.

108

Upon Her Feet

Her pretty feet
    Like snails did creep
A little out, and then,
    As if they started at bo-peep,
Did soon draw in again.

109

His Prayer to Ben Jonson

When I a verse shall make,
    Know I have prayed thee
For old religion's sake,
    Saint Ben, to aid me.

Make the way smooth for me
    When I, thy Herrick,
Honouring thee on my knee
    Offer my lyric.

Candles I'll give to thee,
    And a new altar;
And thou, Saint Ben, shalt be
    Writ in my psalter.

110 ## *To Fortune*

Tumble me down, and I will sit
Upon my ruins, smiling yet;
Tear me to tatters, yet I'll be
Patient in my necessity.
Laugh at my scraps of clothes, and shun
Me, as a feared infection;
Yet scarecrow-like I'll walk, as one
Neglecting thy derision.

111 ## *Lovers, How They Come and Part*

A Gyges' ring they bear about them still,
To be, and not, seen when and where they will.
They tread on clouds, and though they sometimes fall,
They fall like dew, but make no noise at all.
So silently they one to th' other come,
As colours steal into the pear or plum,
And air-like leave no pression to be seen
Where'er they met, or parting place has been.

112 ## *Upon Julia's Clothes*

Whenas in silks my Julia goes,
Then, then, methinks, how sweetly flows
That liquefaction of her clothes.

Next, when I cast mine eyes and see
That brave vibration each way free,
O how that glittering taketh me!

111 Gyges' ring] fabled ring of invisibility

113 ## *Kisses Loathsome*

I abhor the slimy kiss,
Which to me most loathsome is.
Those lips please me which are placed
Close, but not too strictly laced;
Yielding I would have them, yet
Not a wimbling tongue admit.
What should poking-sticks make there,
When the ruff is set elsewhere?

114 ## *To His Book*

Before the press scarce one could see
A little peeping-part of thee;
But since th' art printed, thou dost call
To show thy nakedness to all.
My care for thee is now the less,
Having resigned thy shamefastness;
Go with thy faults and fates; yet stay
And take this sentence, then away:
Whom one beloved will not suffice,
She'll run to all adulteries.

115 ## *His Desire*

Give me a man that is not dull
When all the world with rifts is full,
But unamazed dares clearly sing
Whenas the roof's a-tottering,
And, though it falls, continues still
Tickling the cittern with his quill.

115 cittern] kind of lute played with a plectrum

116 *No Coming to God Without Christ*

Good and great God! How should I fear
To come to Thee, if Christ not there!
Could I but think He would not be
Present to plead my cause for me,
To Hell I'd rather run than I
Would see Thy face, and He not by.

FRANCIS QUARLES

1592–1644

117 *Of Common Devotion*

Our God and soldiers we alike adore,
Even at the brink of danger, not before:
After deliverance, both alike requited,
Our God's forgotten, and our soldiers slighted.

118 *On Zacchaeus*

Methinks I see with what a busy haste
Zacchaeus climbed the tree; but O, how fast,
How full of speed, canst thou imagine, when
Our Saviour called, he powdered down again!
He ne'er made trial if the boughs were sound
Or rotten, nor how far 'twas to the ground;
There was no danger feared; at such a call
He'll venture nothing that dare fear a fall:
Needs must he down, by such a spirit driven,
Nor could he fall unless he fell to Heaven.
Down came Zacchaeus, ravished from the tree:
Bird that was shot ne'er dropped so quick as he.

118 powdered] rushed

119 *On Change of Weathers*

And were it for thy profit, to obtain
All sunshine? No vicissitude of rain?
Think'st thou that thy laborious plough requires
Not winter frosts as well as summer fires?
There must be both: sometimes these hearts of ours
Must have the sweet, the seasonable showers
Of tears; sometimes the frost of chill despair
Makes our desired sunshine seem more fair;
Weathers that most oppose the flesh and blood
Are such as help to make our harvest good.
We may not choose, great God: it is thy task;
We know not what to have, nor how to ask.

HENRY KING

1592–1669

120 Sic Vita

Like to the falling of a star,
Or as the flights of eagles are,
Or like the fresh spring's gaudy hue,
Or silver drops of morning dew,
Or like a wind that chafes the flood,
Or bubbles which on water stood:
Even such is man, whose borrowed light
Is straight called in, and paid to night.

The wind blows out, the bubble dies,
The spring entombed in autumn lies,
The dew dries up, the star is shot,
The flight is past, and man forgot.

120 title] Such Is Life

121 *Sonnet*

Go, thou that vainly dost mine eyes invite
To taste the softer comforts of the night,
And bid'st me cool the fever of my brain
In those sweet balmy dews which slumber pain;
Enjoy thine own peace in untroubled sleep,
Whilst my sad thoughts eternal vigils keep.

O couldst thou for a time change breasts with me,
Thou in that broken glass shouldst plainly see
A heart which wastes in the slow smothering fire
Blown by Despair and fed by false Desire,
Can only reap such sleeps as seamen have,
When fierce winds rock them on the foaming wave.

WILLIAM CAVENDISH, DUKE OF NEWCASTLE

1592–1676

122 *Song*

from *The Humorous Lovers*

We'll, placed in Love's triumphant chariot high,
Be drawn by milkwhite turtles through the sky,
And have for footmen Cupids running by.

A poet coachman, with celestial fire,
His gentle whip of melting pure desire,
Shall drive us while I do thy eyes admire.

Imperial laurel deck our temples round—
As victors, or as heated poets crowned,
Scorning to have commerce with the dull ground!

122 turtles] turtle-doves

Thus we will drive o'er mighty hills of snow,
Viewing poor mortal lovers there below,
Wretches, alas! that know not where we go.

123   *Love's Epitaph*

My epitaph write on your heart,
Since we did part,
For I dare swear I once lay there,
I was so near;
But time that all things doth consume,
I now presume,
Hath wasted me, so that I'm gone,
Both flesh and bone,
And every letter without doubt
Is quite rased out:
Next lover may he be love-curst
As I, the first.

GEORGE HERBERT

1593–1633

124   *Sin*

O that I could a sin once see!
We paint the Devil foul, yet he
Hath some good in him, all agree.
Sin is flat opposite to th' Almighty, seeing
It wants the good of Virtue, and of Being.

But God more care of us has had:
If apparitions make us sad,
By sight of sin we should grow mad.
Yet as in sleep we see foul Death and live,
So devils are our sins in pèrspective.

125 ## *Church Music*

Sweetest of sweets, I thank you: when displeasure
    Did through my body wound my mind,
You took me thence, and in your house of pleasure
    A dainty lodging me assigned.

Now I in you without a body move,
    Rising and falling with your wings;
We both together sweetly live and love,
    Yet say sometimes, 'God help poor kings.'

Comfort, I'll die; for if you post from me,
    Sure I shall do so, and much more;
But if I travel in your company,
    You know the way to Heaven's door.

126 ## *Church Lock and Key*

I know it is my sin which locks thine ears
    And binds thy hands,
Out-crying my requests, drowning my tears;
Or else the chillness of my faint demands.

But as cold hands are angry with the fire,
    And mend it still,
So I do lay the want of my desire
Not on my sins, or coldness, but thy will.

Yet hear, O God, only for his blood's sake
    Which pleads for me:
For though sins plead too, yet like stones they make
His blood's sweet current much more loud to be.

127 ## *Trinity Sunday*

Lord, who hast formed me out of mud,
    And hast redeemed me through thy blood,
    And sanctified me to do good,

Purge all my sins done heretofore;
For I confess my heavy score,
And I will strive to sin no more.

Enrich my heart, mouth, hands, in me
With faith, with hope, with charity,
That I may run, rise, rest, with thee.

128 ### *Bitter-Sweet*

Ah my dear angry Lord,
Since thou dost love, yet strike;
Cast down, yet help afford;
Sure I will do the like.

I will complain, yet praise;
I will bewail, approve;
And all my sour-sweet days
I will lament, and love.

129 ### *A Wreath*

A wreathèd garland of deservèd praise,
Of praise deservèd, unto thee I give,
I give to thee, who knowest all my ways,
My crooked winding ways, wherein I live,
Wherein I die, not live; for life is straight,
Straight as a line, and ever tends to thee,
To thee, who art more far above deceit
Than deceit seems above simplicity.
Give me simplicity, that I may live,
So live and like, that I may know, thy ways,
Know them and practise them: then shall I give
For this poor wreath, give thee a crown of praise.

THOMAS CAREW
1595–1639

130   *Lips and Eyes*

In Celia's face a question did arise:
Which were more beautiful, her lips or eyes.
'We,' said the eyes, 'send forth those pointed darts
Which pierce the hardest adamantine hearts.'
'From us,' replied the lips, 'proceed those blisses
Which lovers reap by kind words and sweet kisses.'
Then wept the eyes, and from their springs did pour
Of liquid oriental pearl a shower,
Whereat the lips, moved with delight and pleasure,
Through a sweet smile unlocked their pearly treasure,
And bade Love judge whether did add more grace
Weeping or smiling pearls to Celia's face.

131   *A Lady's Prayer to Cupid*

Since I must needs into thy school return,
Be pitiful, O Love, and do not burn
Me with desire of cold and frozen age,
Nor let me follow a fond boy or page;
But, gentle Cupid, give me if you can
One to my love, whom I may call a man,
Of person comely, and of face as sweet;
Let him be sober, secret, and discreet,
Well practised in Love's school; let him within
Wear all his beard, and none upon his chin.

131 fond] foolish, doting

57

JAMES SHIRLEY
1596–1666

132   *Song to the Masquers*

from *The Triumph of Peace*

Why do you dwell so long in clouds,
    And smother your best graces?
'Tis time to cast away those shrouds,
    And clear your manly faces.
Do not behave yourselves like spies
    Upon the ladies here;
On even terms go meet their eyes,
    Beauty and Love shine there.
You tread dull measures thus alone,
    Not satisfy delight;
Go kiss their hands and make your own
    With every touch more white.

133   *Fie on Love*

Now, fie on foolish love! It not befits
    Or man or woman know it;
Love was not meant for people in their wits,
    And they that fondly show it
Betray the straw and feathers in their brain,
And shall have Bedlam for their pain.
If single love be such a curse,
To marry is to make it ten times worse.

EDWARD MAY

fl. 1633

134   *On a Young Man and an Old Man*

A young man and an agèd man of late,
Being in a tavern, fell at great debate:
The youth thinking the testy fire to cool
Said, 'Turd i' thy teeth, thou crabbèd doting fool.'
At this the old man laughed, and made reply,
'Turd in his teeth that has teeth, none have I!'
So showed his gums, which made the young man laugh;
They both grew friends, and drank their liquor off.

WILLIAM STRODE

1602–1645

135   *On a Gentlewoman Walking in the Snow*

I saw fair Chloris walk alone
Where feathered rain came softly down,
And Jove descended from his tower
To court her in a silver shower;
The wanton snow flew to her breast
Like little birds into their nest,
And overcome with whiteness there
For grief it thawed into a tear,
Thence falling on her garment's hem
For grief it freezed into a gem.

MILDMAY FANE, EARL OF WESTMORLAND
1602–1665

136 *Occasioned by Seeing a Walk of Bay Trees*

No thunder blasts Jove's plant, nor can
Misfortune warp an honest man;
Shaken he may be, by some one
Or other gust, unleaved by none;
Though tribulation's sharp and keen,
His resolutions keep green;
And whilst integrity's his wall,
His year's all spring, and hath no fall.

137 *In Praise of Fidelia*

Get thee a ship well-rigged and tight,
With ordnance store, and manned for fight,
Snug in her timbers' mould for the seas,
Yet large in hold for merchandise;
Spread forth her cloth, and anchors weigh,
And let her on the curled waves play,
Till, fortune-towed, she chance to meet
Th' Hesperian home-bound Western Fleet;
Then let her board 'em, and for price
Take gold ore, sugar-canes, and spice:
   Yet when all these she hath brought ashore,
   In my Fidelia I'll find more.

138 ## In Obitum Ben. Jons.

He who began from brick and lime
    The Muses' hill to climb,
And, whilom busièd in laying stone,
    Thirsted to drink of Helicon,
    Changing his trowel for a pen,
Wrote straight the temper not of dirt but men.

Now since that he is turned to clay and gone,
    Let those, remain of th' occupation
He honoured once square him a tomb and say
His craft exceeded far a dauber's way.
Then write upon't: He could no longer tarry,
But was returned again unto the quarry.

THOMAS RANDOLPH
1605–1635

139 ### 'Come from thy palace'
from The Conceited Pedlar

Come from thy palace, beauteous queen of Greece,
Sweet Helen of the world. Rise like the morn,
Clad in the smock of night, that all the stars
May lose their eyes, and then, grown blind,
Run weeping to the man i' th' moon
To borrow his dog to lead the spheres a-begging.
Rare empress of our souls, whose charcoal flames
Burn the poor coltsfoot of amazèd hearts,
View the dumb audience thy beauty spies,
And then, amazed with grief, laugh out thine eyes.

138 title] Epitaph on Ben Jonson   those] those who
139 coltsfoot] herb burnt and inhaled medicinally

140 *A Song*

Music, thou queen of souls, get up and string
Thy powerful lute, and some sad requiem sing,
Till rocks requite thy echo with a groan,
And the dull cliffs repeat the duller tone.
Then on a sudden with a nimble hand
Run gently o'er the chords, and so command
The pine to dance, the oak his roots forgo,
The holm and aged elm to foot it too;
Myrtles shall caper, lofty cedars run,
And call the courtly palm to make up one.
Then, in the midst of all their jolly train,
Strike a sad note, and fix 'em trees again.

141 *'From witty men and mad'*

From witty men and mad
All poetry conception had.

No sires but these will poetry admit:
Madness or wit.

This definition poetry doth fit:
It is a witty madness or mad wit!

Only these two poetic heat admits:
A witty man, or one that's out of's wits.

SIR WILLIAM DAVENANT
1606–1668

142   *Song*

The lark now leaves his watery nest,
    And climbing shakes his dewy wings;
He takes this window for the east,
    And to implore your light he sings.
Awake, awake, the morn will never rise
Till she can dress her beauty at your eyes.

The merchant bows unto the seaman's star,
    The ploughman from the sun his season takes;
But still the lover wonders what they are
    Who look for day before his mistress wakes.
Awake, awake, break through your veils of lawn,
Then draw your curtains, and begin the dawn!

SIR WILLIAM BERKELEY
1606?–1677

143   *Song*

from *The Lost Lady*

Where did you borrow that last sigh,
    And that relenting groan?
For those that sigh, and not for love,
    Usurp what's not their own.

Love's arrows sooner armour pierce
    Than your soft snowy skin;
Your eyes can only teach us love,
    But cannot take it in.

EDMUND WALLER
1606–1687

144   *To One Married to an Old Man*

Since thou wouldst needs, bewitched with some ill charms,
Be buried in those monumental arms,
All we can wish is, may that earth lie light
Upon thy tender limbs, and so good-night.

145   *To Chloris, Upon a Favour Received*

Chloris, since first our calm of peace
Was frighted hence, this good we find:
Your favours with your fears increase,
And growing mischiefs make you kind.
So the fair tree, which still preserves
Her fruit and state while no wind blows,
In storms from that uprightness swerves,
And the glad earth about her strows
With treasure from her yielding boughs.

SIR RICHARD FANSHAWE
1608–1666

146   *Nymph's Song*

from *Il Pastor Fido*

Let us use it whilst we may,
Snatch those joys that haste away.
Earth her winter coat may cast
And renew her beauty past,
But, our winter come, in vain
We solicit spring again;
And when our furrows snow shall cover,
Love may return but never lover.

JOHN MILTON
1608–1674

147   *Song*
                         from *Arcades*

O'er the smooth enamelled green
Where no print of step hath been,
    Follow me as I sing,
    And touch the warbled string.
Under the shady roof
Of branching elm star-proof,
    Follow me:
I will bring you where she sits,
Clad in splendour as befits
    Her deity.
Such a rural queen
All Arcadia hath not seen.

CLEMENT BARKSDALE
1609–1687

148   *To My Nephew, J.B.*

The care thy father once bestowed on me,
I very gladly would return to thee.
What I to thee (thus love in a blood runs)
Do thou communicate unto my sons.
I have no land to give, such is my chance,
Take this poetical inheritance.
A little here is best: because much more
Of poetry, perhaps, would make you poor.

RICHARD CRASHAW
1612?–1649

149   *On the Miracle of Multiplied Loaves*

See here an easy feast that knows no wound,
    That under hunger's teeth will needs be sound;
A subtle harvest of unbounded bread.
    What would ye more? Here food itself is fed.

150   *To the Infant Martyrs*

Go, smiling souls, your new-built cages break;
In Heaven you'll learn to sing ere here to speak.
Nor let the milky fonts that bathe your thirst
        Be your delay:
The place that calls you hence is at the worst
        Milk all the way.

151   *On the Miracle of Loaves*

Now, Lord, or never, they'll believe on thee:
Thou to their teeth hast proved thy Deity.

152   *On the Blessed Virgin's Bashfulness*

That on her lap she casts her humble eye
'Tis the sweet pride of her humility.
The fair star is well fixed, for where, O where
Could she have fixed it on a fairer sphere?
'Tis Heaven, 'tis Heaven she sees, Heaven's God there lies:
She can see Heaven and ne'er lift up her eyes.
This new guest to her eyes new laws hath given:
'Twas once *look up*, 'tis now *look down* to Heaven.

153 *On Our Crucified Lord, Naked and Bloody*

> They have left thee naked, Lord: O that they had;
> This garment too I would they had denied.
> Thee with thy self they have too richly clad,
> Opening the purple wardrobe of thy side.
>> O never could be found garments too good
>> For thee to wear, but these of thine own blood.

JAMES GRAHAM, MARQUIS OF MONTROSE

1612–1650

154 *On Himself, Upon Hearing What Was His Sentence*

> Let them bestow on every airth a limb;
> Open all my veins, that I may swim
> To thee my Saviour in that crimson lake;
> Then place my parboiled head upon a stake,
> Scatter my ashes, throw them in the air.
> Lord, since thou know'st where all these atoms are,
> I'm hopeful once thou'lt recollect my dust,
> And confident thou'lt raise me with the just.

154 airth] quarter of the compass   once] at some time

ANNE BRADSTREET

1612?–1672

155   *To My Dear and Loving Husband*

If ever two were one, then surely we.
If ever man were loved by wife, then thee;
If ever wife was happy in a man,
Compare with me, ye women, if you can.
I prize thy love more than whole mines of gold,
Or all the riches that the East doth hold.
My love is such that rivers cannot quench,
Nor aught but love from thee give recompense.
Thy love is such I can no way repay;
The heavens reward thee manifold, I pray.
Then while we live, in love let's so persever,
That when we live no more we may live ever.

ROBERT HEATH

(*fl.* 1650)

156   *Seeing Her Dancing*

Robes loosely flowing and aspect as free,
A careless carriage decked with modesty;
    A smiling look, but yet severe:
    Such comely graces about her were.

Her steps with such an evenness she wove
As she could hardly be perceived to move;
    Whilst, her silk sails displayèd, she
    Swam like a ship with majesty.

As when with steadfast eyes we view the sun
We know it goes though see no motion;
    So undiscerned she moved, that we
    Perceived she stirred, but did not see.

SIR JOHN DENHAM
1615–1669

157   *Preface to* The Progress of Learning

My early Mistress, now my ancient Muse,
That strong Circean liquor cease to infuse,
Wherewith thou didst intoxicate my youth;
Now stoop with disenchanted wings to truth.
As the dove's flight did guide Aeneas, now
May thine conduct me to the Golden Bough:
Tell, like a tall old oak, how learning shoots
To Heaven her branches and to Hell her roots.

GEORGE DANIEL
1616–1657

158 *One Desiring Me to Read, but Slept It Out,*
                   Wakening

Nay do not smile: my lips shall rather dwell
    For ever on my pipe
Than read to you one word or syllable.
    You are not ripe
To judge or apprehend
Of wit. I'll rather spend
Six hours together in tobacco-taking,
Than read to you, and cannot keep you waking.

RICHARD LOVELACE
1618–1658

159   *To Lucasta, Going to the Wars*

Tell me not, sweet, I am unkind,
    That from the nunnery
Of thy chaste breast and quiet mind
    To war and arms I fly.

True, a new mistress now I chase,
    The first foe in the field;
And with a stronger faith embrace
    A sword, a horse, a shield.

Yet this inconstancy is such
    As you too shall adore;
I could not love thee, dear, so much,
    Loved I not Honour more.

160   *Song*

In mine own monument I lie,
    And in my self am burièd;
Sure the quick lightning of her eye
    Melted my soul i' the scabbard, dead;
And now like some pale ghost I walk,
And with another's spirit talk.

Nor can her beams a heat convey
    That may my frozen bosom warm,
Unless her smiles have power, as they
    That a cross charm can countercharm;
But this is such a pleasing pain,
    I'm loath to be alive again.

SIR EDWARD SHERBURNE
1618–1702

161   *The Dream*

Fair shadow, faithless as my sun!
　　Of peace she robs my mind,
And to my sense, which rest doth shun,
　　Thou art no less unkind.

She my address disdainful flies,
　　And thou, like her, art fleet;
The real beauty she denies
　　And thou the counterfeit.

To cross my innocent desires
　　And make my griefs extreme,
A cruel mistress thus conspires
　　With a delusive dream.

162   *'The proud Egyptian queen'*

*And she washed his feet with her tears, and wiped them with the
hairs of her head.*

The proud Egyptian queen, her Roman guest
(To express her love in height of state and pleasure)
　　With pearl dissolved in gold did feast:
　　　　Both food and treasure.

And now, dear Lord, thy lover, on the fair
And silver tables of thy feet, behold!
　　Pearl in her tears, and in her hair
　　　　Offers thee gold.

RICHARD FLECKNOE

?–1678

163   *Invocation of Silence*

Still-born Silence, thou that art
Flood-gate of the deeper heart!
Offspring of a heavenly kind,
Frost o' the mouth, and thaw o' the mind,
Secrecy's confidant, and he
Who makes religion mystery!
Admiration's speakingest tongue!
Leave, thy desert shades among,
Reverend hermits' hallowed cells
Where retired Devotion dwells!
With thy enthusiasms come,
Seize our tongues, and strike us dumb!

HENRY VAUGHAN

1622–1695

164   *The Eclipse*

Whither, O whither didst thou fly
When I did grieve thine holy eye,
When thou didst mourn to see me lost,
And all thy care and counsels crossed?
O do not grieve where'er thou art!
Thy grief is an undoing smart,
Which doth not only pain, but break
My heart, and makes me blush to speak.
Thy anger I could kiss, and will:
But O! thy grief, thy grief doth kill.

MARGARET CAVENDISH,
DUCHESS OF NEWCASTLE
1624–1674

165 ### *Soul and Body*

Great Nature she doth clothe the soul within
A fleshly garment which the Fates do spin.
And when these garments are grown old and bare,
With sickness torn, Death takes them off with care,
And folds them up in peace and quiet rest,
And lays them safe within an earthly chest;
Then scours them, and makes them sweet and clean,
Fit for the soul to wear those clothes again.

166 ### *Of the Theme of Love*

O Love, how thou art tired out with rhyme!
Thou art a tree whereon all poets climb;
And from thy branches every one takes some
Of thy sweet fruit, which fancy feeds upon.
But now thy tree is left so bare and poor
That they can hardly gather one plum more.

JOHN HALL
1627–1656

167 ### *Song*

Distil not poison in mine ears,
    Aërial sirens, nor untie
These sable fetters! Yonder spheres
    Dance to a silent harmony.

Could I but follow where you lead,
   Disrobed of earth and plumed by air,
Then I my tenuous self might spread
   As quick as fancy everywhere.

But I'll make sallies now and then:
   Thus can my unconfinèd eye
Take journey and return again,
   Yet on her crystal couch still lie.

JOHN BUNYAN
1628–1688

168   *Song of the Shepherd Boy*

from *The Pilgrim's Progress*

He that is down needs fear no fall,
   He that is low, no pride:
He that is humble ever shall
   Have God to be his guide.

I am content with what I have,
   Little it be, or much:
And Lord, contentment still I crave,
   Because thou savest such.

Fullness to such a burden is
   That go on pilgrimage;
Here little, and hereafter bliss,
   Is best from age to age.

169   *Upon the Snail*

She goes but softly, but she goeth sure;
   She stumbles not as stronger creatures do:
Her journey's shorter, so she may endure
   Better than they which do much further go.

JOHN BUNYAN

She makes no noise, but stilly seizeth on
  The flower or herb appointed for her food,
The which she quietly doth feed upon,
  While others range, and gare, but find no good.

And though she doth but very softly go,
  However 'tis not fast, nor slow, but sure;
And certainly they that do travel so,
  The prize they do aim at they do procure.

KATHERINE PHILIPS
1631–1664

170 *Song*

  'Tis true our life is but a long dis-ease,
  Made up of real pain and seeming ease.
  You stars, who these entangled fortunes give,
      O tell me why
      It is so hard to die,
        Yet such a task to live?

  If with some pleasure we our griefs betray,
  It costs us dearer than it can repay.
  For time or fortune all things so devours,
      Our hopes are crossed,
      Or else the object lost,
        Ere we can call it ours.

169 gare] stare about

75

JOHN DRYDEN
1631–1700

171   *Mercury's Song*

from *Amphitryon*

Fair Iris I love, and hourly I die,
But not for a lip nor a languishing eye:
She's fickle and false, and there we agree,
But I am as false and as fickle as she;
We neither believe what either can say,
And, neither believing, we neither betray.

'Tis civil to swear and say things of course;
We mean not the taking for better for worse.
When present, we love; when absent, agree:
I think not of Iris, nor Iris of me.
The legend of love no couple can find
So easy to part, or so equally joined.

172   *Momus' Song to Mars*

from *The Secular Masque*

Thy sword within the scabbard keep,
    And let mankind agree;
Better the world were fast asleep
    Than kept awake by thee.
The fools are only thinner
    With all our cost and care;
But neither side a winner,
    For things are as they were.

JOHN DRYDEN

173

Chorus to the Gods

from *The Secular Masque*

All, all of a piece throughout:
Thy chase had a beast in view;
Thy wars brought nothing about;
Thy lovers were all untrue.
'Tis well an old age is out,
And time to begin a new.

PHILIP PAIN

*?–c.*1666

174

Meditation 8

Scarce do I pass a day but that I hear
Some one or other's dead, and to my ear
Methinks it is no news. But oh! did I
Think deeply on it, what it is to die,
    My pulses all would beat, I should not be
    Drowned in this deluge of security.

THOMAS TRAHERNE

1637–1674

175

Christian Ethics

All music, sauces, feasts, delights and pleasures,
Games, dancing, arts, consist in governed measures;
Much more do words, and passions of the mind,
In temperance their sacred beauty find.

THOMAS FLATMAN
1637–1688

176   Nudus Redibo

Naked I came when I began to be
A man among the sons of misery,
Tender, unarmed, helpless and quite forlorn,
E'er since 'twas my hard fortune to be born;
And when the space of a few weary days
Shall be expired, then must I go my ways.
Naked I shall return, and nothing have:
Nothing wherewith to bribe my hungry grave.
Then what's the proudest monarch's glittering robe,
Or what's he more than I that ruled the globe,
Since we must all without distinction die,
And slumber both stark naked, he and I?

CHARLES SACKVILLE, EARL OF DORSET
1638–1706

177   *On Dorinda*

Dorinda's sparkling wit and eyes,
United, cast too fierce a light,
Which blazes high, but quickly dies,
Pains not the heart, but hurts the sight.

Love is a calmer, gentler joy:
Smooth are his looks, and soft his pace;
Her Cupid is a blackguard boy
That runs his link full in your face.

176 title] Naked I Shall Return
177 link] flaming torch

PHILIP AYRES
1638–1712

178   *Ever Present*

Her name is at my tongue whene'er I speak,
  Her shape's before my eyes where'er I stir,
Both day and night, as if her ghost did walk,
  And not she me, but I had murdered her.

ANONYMOUS
(late 17th century)

179   *The Old Man's Complaint*

Ah, pity love where'er it grows!
See how in me it overflows
In dripping eyes and dropping nose.

So strange a thing is seldom seen:
My age is dull, my love is keen;
Above I'm grey, but elsewhere green.

Aloof, perhaps I court and prate;
But something near I would be at,
Though I'm so old I scarce know what.

180   *A Thought on Human Life*

Some, striving knowledge to refine,
  Consume themselves with thinking;
And some, whose friendship's drowned in wine,
  Are kindly killed with drinking;

And some are wrecked on Indian coasts,
  Thither with gain invited;
And some in smoke of battle lost,
  Whom drums, not lutes, delighted.

JOHN CROWNE
1640?–1703?

181   *Song*

from *Calisto*

Kind lovers, love on,
Lest the world be undone,
And mankind be lost by degrees:
  For if all from their loves
  Should go wander in groves,
There soon would be nothing but trees.

THOMAS RYMER
1641–1713

182   *To* ——

Let those with cost deck their ill-fashioned clay
Who only are with their fine feathers gay,
Whilst you, despising false and borrowed light,
Shine of yourself more gloriously bright.
Whatever art can make, or wit invent,
Would be on you superfluously spent;
Your beauty needs no ornament or dress,
And would be made by all additions less.
You still triumph amidst your marriage toil,

80

And make the brightest virgin but your foil;
Still in its bloom you keep your maiden pride,
And spite of all your children seem a bride.

JOHN WILMOT, EARL OF ROCHESTER
1647–1680

183   *To My More than Meritorious Wife*

I am, by fate, slave to your will
And shall be most obedient still.
To show my love, I will compose ye,
For your fair finger's ring, a posy,
In which shall be expressed my duty,
And how I'll be forever true t'ye.
With low-made legs and sugared speeches,
Yielding to your fair bum the breeches,
I'll show myself, in all I can,
Your faithful, humble servant,
                                        John.

184   *Grecian Kindness*

The utmost grace the Greeks could show,
    When to the Trojans they grew kind,
Was with their arms to let 'em go
    And leave their lingering wives behind.
They beat the men, and burnt the town:
Then all the baggage was their own.

There the kind deity of wine
    Kissed the soft wanton god of love;
This clapped his wings, that pressed his vine,
    And their best powers united move;
While each brave Greek embraced his punk,
Lulled her asleep, and then grew drunk.

184 grace] mercy   punk] whore

81

185 *Song*

Leave this gaudy gilded stage,
　From custom more than use frequented,
Where fools of either sex and age
　Crowd to see themselves presented.

To love's theatre, the bed,
　Youth and beauty fly together,
And act so well it may be said
　The laurel there was due to either.

'Twixt strifes of love and war the difference lies in this:
When neither overcomes, love's triumph greater is.

186 *A Rodomontade on His Cruel Mistress*

Trust not that thing called woman: she is worse
Than all ingredients crammed into a curse.
Were she but ugly, peevish, proud, a whore,
Poxed, painted, perjured, so she were no more,
I could forgive her, and connive at this,
Alleging still she but a woman is.
But she is worse: in time she will forestall
The Devil, and be the damning of us all.

HENRY ALDRICH
1647–1710

187 *A Catch*

If all be true that I do think,
There are five reasons we should drink:
Good wine, a friend, or being dry,
Or lest we should be by and by,
Or any other reason why.

NAHUM TATE
1652–1715

The Choice

Grant me, indulgent Heaven, a rural seat,
    Rather contemptible than great;
Where, though I taste life's sweets, still I may be
    Athirst for immortality.
I would have business, but exempt from strife;
    A private, but an active, life;
A conscience bold, and punctual to his charge;
    My stock of health, or patience, large.
Some books I'd have, and some acquaintance too,
    But very good, and very few.
Then (if one mortal two such grants may crave)
    From silent life I'd steal into my grave.

JANE BARKER
(*fl.* 1688)

To Her Lover's Complaint

If you complain your flames are hot,
    'Tis 'cause they are impure:
For strongest spirits scorch us not,
    Their flames we can endure.

Love, like zeal, should be divine,
    And ardent as the same:
Like stars, which in cold weather shine,
    Or like a lambent flame.

It should be like the morning rays
    Which quickens, but not burns;
Or th' innocence of children's plays,
    Or lamps in ancient urns.

SIR GEORGE ETHEREGE
1653–1691

190   *Song*

from *The Comical Revenge*

Ladies, though to your conquering eyes
Love owes his chiefest victories,
And borrows those bright arms from you
With which he does the world subdue,
    Yet you yourselves are not above
    The empire nor the griefs of love.

Then wrack not lovers with disdain,
Lest Love on you revenge their pain;
You are not free because you're fair:
The boy did not his mother spare.
    Beauty's but an offensive dart;
    It is no armour for the heart.

ANNE FINCH, COUNTESS OF WINCHILSEA
1661?–1720

191   *On Myself*

Good heaven, I thank thee, since it was designed
I should be framed but of the weaker kind,
That yet my soul is rescued from the love
Of all those trifles which their passions move.
Pleasures, and praise, and plenty, have with me
But their just value. If allowed they be,
Freely and thankfully as much I taste
As will not reason or religion waste.
If they're denied, I on myself can live,
And slight those aids unequal chance does give:
When in the sun, my wings can be displayed;
And in retirement I can bless the shade.

192

A Song

The nymph in vain bestows her pains,
That seeks to thrive where Bacchus reigns;
In vain are charms, or smiles, or frowns,
All images his torrent drowns.

Flames to the head he may impart,
But makes an island of the heart;
So inaccessible and cold,
That to be his is to be old.

WILLIAM WALSH
1663–1708

193

To His False Mistress

Thou saidst that I alone thy heart could move,
And that for me thou wouldst abandon Jove.
I loved thee then, nor with a love defiled,
But as a father loves his only child.
I know thee now, and though I fiercelier burn,
Thou art become the object of my scorn.
See what thy falsehood gets: I must confess
I love thee more, but I esteem thee less.

194

Phillis's Resolution

When slaves their liberties require
They hope no more to gain,
But you not only that desire
But ask the power to reign.

Think how unjust a suit you make,
Then you will soon decline;
Your freedom, when you please, pray take,
But trespass not on mine.

No more in vain, Alcander, crave;
I ne'er will grant the thing,
That he who once has been my slave
Should ever be my king.

MATTHEW PRIOR

1664–1721

195   Les Estreines

Accept, my love, as true a heart
    As ever lover gave:
'Tis free, it vows, from any art,
    And proud to be your slave.

Then take it kindly, as 'twas meant,
    And let the giver live,
Who, with it, would the world have sent,
    Had it been his to give.

And, that Dorinda may not fear
    I e'er will prove untrue,
My vows shall, ending with the year,
    With it begin anew.

196   Adriani Morientis ad Animam Suam

Poor little, pretty, fluttering thing,
    Must we no longer live together?
And dost thou prune thy trembling wing,
    To take thy flight thou know'st not whither?

Thy humorous vein, thy pleasing folly,
    Lies all neglected, all forgot:
And pensive, wavering, melancholy,
    Thou dread'st and hop'st thou know'st not what.

195 title] A New Year's Gift
196 title] Hadrian Dying, to His Soul (lines by the Roman emperor Hadrian)

197 *The Lady Who Offers Her Looking-Glass*
to Venus

Venus, take my votive glass:
Since I am not what I was,
What from this day I shall be,
Venus, let me never see.

198 *Democritus and Heraclitus*

Democritus, dear droll, revisit Earth,
And with our follies glut thy heightened mirth.
Sad Heraclitus, serious wretch, return,
In louder grief our greater crimes to mourn.
Between you both I unconcerned stand by:
Hurt, can I laugh? and honest, need I cry?

199 *A Letter to the Honourable Lady,*
Miss Margaret Cavendish-Holles-Harley

My noble, lovely, little Peggy,
Let this, my First Epistle, beg ye,
At dawn of morn, and close of even,
To lift your heart and hands to Heaven.
In double beauty say your prayer:
'Our Father' first, then 'Notre Père';
And, dearest child, along the day,
In every thing you do and say,
Obey and please my Lord and Lady,
So God shall love, and angels aid ye.

If to these precepts you attend,
No Second Letter need I send,
And so I rest your constant friend,
                                        M.P.

200 *The Insatiable Priest*

Luke Preach-Ill admires what we laymen can mean,
   That thus by our profit and pleasure are swayed;
He has but three livings, and would be a Dean;
   His wife died this year, he has married his maid.

To suppress all his carnal desires in their birth,
   At all hours a lusty young hussy is near;
And to take off his thought from the things of this earth,
   He can be content with two thousand a year.

GEORGE GRANVILLE, LORD LANSDOWNE

1667–1735

201 *'Impatient with desire'*

Impatient with desire, at last
   I ventured to lay forms aside;
'Twas I was modest, not she chaste:
   The nymph as soon as asked complied.

With amorous awe, a silent fool,
   I gazed upon her eyes with fear;
Speak, Love, how came your slave so dull
   To read no better there?

Thus, to ourselves the greatest foes
   Although the fair be well inclined,
For want of courage to propose,
   By our own folly she's unkind.

Cloe

202

Cloe's the wonder of her sex,
  'Tis well her heart is tender;
How might such killing eyes perplex,
  With virtue to defend her?

But Nature, graciously inclined
  With liberal hand to please us,
Has to her boundless beauty joined
  A boundless bent to ease us.

JONATHAN SWIFT
1667–1745

Shall I Repine?

203

If neither brass nor marble can withstand
The mortal force of Time's destructive hand;
If mountains sink to vales, if cities die,
And lessening rivers mourn their fountains dry,
'When my old cassock,' says a Welsh divine,
'Is out at elbows, why should I repine?'

WILLIAM CONGREVE
1670–1729

Song

204

See, see, she wakes, Sabina wakes!
  And now the sun begins to rise;
Less glorious is the morn that breaks
  From his bright beams than her fair eyes.

With light united, day they give,
　But different fates ere night fulfil.
How many by his warmth will live!
How many will her coldness kill!

205　　　　　　　*Song*

　Pious Selinda goes to prayers
　　If I but ask the favour;
　And yet the tender fool's in tears
　　When she believes I'll leave her.

　Would I were free from this restraint,
　　Or else had hopes to win her;
　Would she could make of me a saint,
　　Or I of her a sinner.

206　　　　　　　*Lesbia*

When Lesbia first I saw so heavenly fair,
With eyes so bright, and with that aweful air,
I thought my heart, which durst so high aspire,
As bold as his who snatched celestial fire.
But soon as e'er the beauteous idiot spoke,
Forth from her coral lips such folly broke,
Like balm the trickling nonsense healed my wound,
And what her eyes enthralled her tongue unbound.

207　　　　　　　*Song*

　False though she be to me and Love,
　　I'll ne'er pursue revenge;
　For still the charmer I approve,
　　Though I deplore her change.

　In hours of bliss we oft have met—
　　They could not always last;
　And though the present I regret,
　　I'm grateful for the past.

JONATHAN SMEDLEY
1671–1729?

208

Fancy
A Madrigal

'Twas fancy first made Celia fair,
'Twas fancy gave her shape and air.
It robbed the sun, stripped every star
Of beauties to bestow on her:
And, when it had the goddess made,
Down it fell, and worshippèd.

Creator first, and then a creature!
Narcissus! and a pail of water!

SIR RICHARD STEELE
1672–1729

209

Trim's Song: The Fair Kitchen-Maid
from *The Funeral*

Cynderaxa kind and good
    Has all my heart and stomach too:
She makes me love, not hate, my food,
    As other peevish wenches do.

When Venus leaves her Vulcan's cell,
    Which all but I a coal-hole call,
Fly, fly, ye that above stairs dwell:
    Her face is washed, ye vanish all.

And as she's fair, she can impart
    That beauty to make all things fine:
Brightens the floor with wondrous art,
    And at her touch the dishes shine.

91

ESTHER JOHNSON
1681–1728

210   *'If it be true'*

If it be true, celestial Powers,
    That you have formed me fair,
And yet in all my vainest hours
    My mind has been my care;
Then in return I beg this grace,
    As you were ever kind:
What envious Time takes from my face,
    Bestow upon my mind.

211   *Jealousy*

Oh, shield me from his rage, celestial Powers!
This tyrant that embitters all my hours.
Ah! Love, you've poorly played the monarch's part:
You conquered, but you can't defend, my heart.
So blessed was I throughout thy happy reign,
I thought this monster banished from thy train;
But you would raise him to support your throne,
And now he claims your empire as his own:
Or tell me, tyrants, have you both agreed
That where one reigns the other shall succeed?

JOHN GAY
1685–1732

212   *Song*

from *The Beggar's Opera*

Can love be controlled by advice?
    Will Cupid our mothers obey?
Though my heart was as frozen as ice,
    At his flame 'twould have melted away.

JOHN GAY

When he kissed me, so closely he pressed,
    'Twas so sweet that I must have complied;
So I thought it both safest and best
    To marry, for fear you should chide.

213   *Song*

             from *The Beggar's Opera*

Before the barn-door crowing,
    The cock by hens attended,
His eyes around him throwing,
    Stands for a while suspended:
Then one he singles from the crew
    And cheers the happy hen,
With how do you do, and how do you do,
    And how do you do again.

214   *Song*

                from *Achilles*

    Think of dress in every light:
        'Tis woman's chiefest duty;
    Neglecting that, ourselves we slight,
        And undervalue beauty.
    That allures the lover's eye,
        And graces every action:
    Besides, when not a creature's by
        'Tis inward satisfaction.

JOHN GAY

When he kissed me, so closely he pressed,
    'Twas so sweet that I must have complied;
So I thought it both safest and best
    To marry, for fear you should chide.

213   *Song*

             from *The Beggar's Opera*

Before the barn-door crowing,
    The cock by hens attended,
His eyes around him throwing,
    Stands for a while suspended:
Then one he singles from the crew
    And cheers the happy hen,
With how do you do, and how do you do,
    And how do you do again.

214   *Song*

                from *Achilles*

    Think of dress in every light:
        'Tis woman's chiefest duty;
    Neglecting that, ourselves we slight,
        And undervalue beauty.
    That allures the lover's eye,
        And graces every action:
    Besides, when not a creature's by
        'Tis inward satisfaction.

93

AARON HILL
1685–1750

215   *Written on a Window*

Tender-handed stroke a nettle
  And it stings you for your pains;
Grasp it like a man of mettle
  And it soft as silk remains.

'Tis the same with common natures:
  Use them kindly, they rebel;
But be rough as nutmeg-graters
  And the rogues obey you well.

216   *Modesty*

As lamps burn silent, with unconscious light,
So modest ease, in beauty, shines most bright:
Unaiming charms with edge resistless fall,
And she who means no mischief does it all.

ALEXANDER POPE
1688–1744

217   *On Dullness*

Thus Dullness, the safe opiate of the mind,
The last kind refuge weary Wit can find,
Fit for all stations, and in each content,
Is satisfied, secure, and innocent.
No pains it takes, and no offence it gives:
Unfeared, unhated, undisturbed it lives.
And if each writing author's best pretence
Be but to teach the ignorant more sense,
Then Dullness was the cause they wrote before,
As 'tis at last the cause they write no more.
So Wit, which most to scorn it does pretend,
With Dullness first began, in Dullness last must end.

218   ## On a Lady Who P-ssed at the
                 Tragedy of Cato

While maudlin Whigs deplored their Cato's fate,
Still with dry eyes the Tory Celia sate;
But while her pride forbids her tears to flow,
The gushing waters find a vent below:
Though secret, yet with copious grief she mourns,
Like twenty river-gods with all their urns.
Let others screw their hypocritic face,
She shows her grief in a sincerer place:
There Nature reigns, and Passion void of art,
For that road leads directly to the heart.

219   ## Upon a Girl of Seven Years Old

Wit's queen (if what the poets sing be true)
And Beauty's goddess, childhood never knew—
Pallas, they say, sprung from the head of Jove
Full grown, and from the sea the queen of Love;
But had they, Miss, your wit and beauty seen,
Venus and Pallas both had children been.
They, from the sweetness of that radiant look,
A copy of young Venus might have took,
And from those pretty things you speak have told
How Pallas talked when she was seven years old.

220   ## A Hymn

Written in Windsor Forest

All hail, once pleasing, once inspiring shade,
    Scene of my youthful loves and happier hours,
Where the kind Muses met me as I strayed,
    And gently pressed my hand, and said, 'Be ours!
Take all thou e'er shalt have, a constant Muse:
    At court thou may'st be liked, but nothing gain;
Stocks thou may'st buy and sell, but always lose;
    And love the brightest eyes, but love in vain!'

95

ALEXANDER POPE

221 *On a Certain Lady at Court*

I know the thing that's most uncommon
  (Envy be silent, and attend!),
I know a reasonable woman,
  Handsome and witty, yet a friend.

Not warped by passion, awed by rumour,
  Not grave through pride, or gay through folly,
An equal mixture of good humour
  And sensible soft melancholy.

'Has she no faults then (Envy says), sir?'
  Yes, she has one, I must aver:
When all the world conspires to praise her
  The woman's deaf, and does not hear.

222 Inscriptio

And thou! whose sense, whose humour, and whose rage
At once can teach, delight, and lash the age,
Whether thou choose Cervantes' serious air,
Or laugh and shake in Rabelais' easy chair,
Praise courts and monarchs, or extol mankind,
Or thy grieved country's copper chains unbind;
Attend whatever title please thine ear,
Dean, Drapier, Bickerstaff, or Gulliver.
From thy Bœotia, lo! the fog retires,
Yet grieve not thou at what our isle acquires;
Here Dullness reigns, with mighty wings outspread,
And brings the true Saturnian age of lead.

223 *Epigram*

When other ladies to the shades go down,
Still Flavia, Chloris, Celia stay in town;
Those ghosts of beauty lingering there abide,
And haunt the places where their honour died.

222 title] Inscription (written for his friend Dean Swift)

96

224   *To Mr C, St James's Place, London,*
                    October 22nd

> Few words are best; I wish you well;
>   Bethel, I'm told, will soon be here;
> Some morning walks along the Mall,
>   And evening friends, will end the year.
>
> If, in this interval between
>   The falling leaf and coming frost,
> You please to see, on Twickenham Green,
>   Your friend, your poet, and your host,
>
> For three whole days you here may rest
>   From office, business, news, and strife:
> And (what most folks would think a jest)
>   Want nothing else, except your wife.

225   *Epigram*

*Engraved on the Collar of a Dog which I Gave to His Royal
Highness*

> I am his Highness' Dog at Kew:
> Pray tell me, sir, whose dog are you?

226 *On the Benefactions in the Late Frost, 1740*

> 'Yes, 'tis the time,' I cried, 'impose the chain
>   Destined and due to wretches self-enslaved!'
> But when I saw such charity remain,
>   I half could wish this people might be saved.
> Faith lost, and hope, their charity begins;
>   And 'tis a wise design on pitying Heaven,
> If this can cover multitudes of sins,
>   To take the only way to be forgiven.

LADY MARY WORTLEY MONTAGU
1689–1762

227　　　　　　*The Lady's Resolve*

Whilst thirst of praise, and vain desire of fame,
In every age is every woman's aim,
With courtship pleased, of silly toasters proud,
Fond of a train, and happy in a crowd,
On each poor fool bestowing some kind glance,
Each conquest owing to some loose advance,
Whilst vain coquettes affect to be pursued,
And think they're virtuous if not grossly lewd;
Let this great maxim be my virtue's guide:
In part she is to blame that has been tried;
He comes too near that comes to be denied.

SAMUEL WESLEY
1691–1739

228　　　　　　*The Monument*

A monster, in a course of vice grown old,
Leaves to his gaping heir his ill-gained gold:
Straight breathes his bust, straight are his virtues shown,
Their date commencing with the sculptured stone.
If on his specious marble we rely,
Pity a worth like his should ever die!
If credit to his real life we give,
Pity a wretch like him should ever live!

ANONYMOUS (attr. Samuel Wesley)

229 *On the Setting Up Mr Butler's Monument in Westminster Abbey*

While Butler, needy wretch, was yet alive,
No generous patron would a dinner give;
See him, when starved to death and turned to dust,
Presented with a monumental bust!
The poet's fate is here in emblem shown:
He asked for bread, and he received a stone.

THOMAS FITZGERALD
1695?–1752

230   *Upon an Ingenious Friend, Over-Vain*

Dear Frank, with fancy, fire and style
    Formed a consummate poet,
Burns with impatience all the while
    That all the world should know it.

Where'er he goes, with pompous boast
    His talent he displays;
No, not a tittle shall be lost
    Of his minutest praise!

Then let's be candid to our friend,
    And own his just pretence;
Nor yet, whilst we his wit commend,
    Despise his want of sense.

ROBERT DODSLEY
1703–1764

231   *Song*

Man's a poor deluded bubble,
   Wandering in a mist of lies,
Seeing false, or seeing double,
   Who would trust to such weak eyes?
Yet, presuming on his senses,
   On he goes, most wondrous wise:
Doubts of truth, believes pretences,
   Lost in error lives and dies.

WILLIAM PATTISON
1706–1727

232   Ad Coelum

Good Heaven! this mystery of life explain,
Nor let me think I bear the load in vain;
Lest, with the tedious passage cheerless grown,
Urged by despair I throw the burden down.

232 title] To Heaven

JOHN WIGSON

*c.*1711–?

233　*On the Death of Squire Christopher,*
　　　a Remarkably Fat Sportsman

Tired with too long a chase, though stout—
For who can always hold it out?—
Old Christopher—and sure it grieves us—
At last is lagged behind and leaves us;
Has slowly taken Nature's road
And stumbled under his own load;
As true an heart—deny't who dare—
As drank his glass or carved his hare.
Then take the horn, and wind it o'er
The man who loved it so before.
Then let him sleep—and say no more.
Life breeds a throng; and Death must come
To thrust some out, to *make more room*.

WILLIAM SHENSTONE

1714–1763

234　*Lines Written on a Window at The Leasowes*
　　　at a Time of Very Deep Snow

In this small fort, besieged with snow,
When every studious pulse beats low,
　　What does my wish require?
Some sprightly girls beneath my roof,
Some friends sincere and winter-proof,
　　A bottle and a fire.

Prolong, O snow, prolong thy siege!
With these, thou wilt but more oblige,
　　And bless me with thy stay;
Extend, extend thy frigid reign,
My few sincerer friends detain,
　　And keep false friends away.

THOMAS GRAY

1716–1771

235　　　　*Tophet*

Such Tophet was; so looked the grinning fiend
While frighted prelates bowed and called him friend;
I saw them bow, and while they wished him dead
With servile simper nod the mitred head.
Our Mother Church with half-averted sight
Blushed as she blessed her grisly proselyte:
Hosannahs rung through Hell's tremendous borders,
And Satan's self had thoughts of taking orders.

WILLIAM COLLINS

1721–1759

236　　　　*Ode*

Written in the Beginning of the Year 1746

How sleep the brave who sink to rest
By all their country's wishes blest!
When Spring, with dewy fingers cold,
Returns to deck their hallowed mould,
She there shall dress a sweeter sod
Than Fancy's feet have ever trod.

By fairy hands their knell is rung,
By forms unseen their dirge is sung;
There Honour comes, a pilgrim grey,
To bless the turf that wraps their clay;
And Freedom shall awhile repair
To dwell a weeping hermit there!

237 *Sonnet*

When Phoebe formed a wanton smile,
　My soul, it reached not here!
Strange that thy peace, thou trembler, flies
　Before a rising tear!

From midst the drops my love is born,
　That o'er those eyelids rove:
Thus issued from a teeming wave
　The fabled queen of love.

OLIVER GOLDSMITH
1730–1774

238 *'O Memory, thou fond deceiver'*

from *The Captivity*

O Memory, thou fond deceiver,
　Still importunate and vain,
To former joys recurring ever,
　And turning all the past to pain;

Thou, like the world, the oppressed oppressing,
　Thy smiles increase the wretch's woe;
And he who wants each other blessing
　In thee must ever find a foe.

WILLIAM COWPER
1731–1800

239   *A Comparison*

The lapse of time and rivers is the same:
Both speed their journey with a restless stream,
The silent pace with which they steal away
No wealth can bribe, no prayers persuade to stay;
Alike irrevocable both when past,
And a wide ocean swallows both at last.
Though each resemble each in every part,
A difference strikes at length the musing heart:
Streams never flow in vain; where streams abound,
How laughs the land with various plenty crowned!
But time that should enrich the nobler mind,
Neglected, leaves a dreary waste behind.

SIR WILLIAM JONES
1746–1794

240   *A Moral Tetrastich*
                        from the Persian

On parent knees, a naked new-born child,
Weeping thou sat'st when all around thee smiled:
So live, that sinking in thy last long sleep,
Calm thou mayst smile when all around thee weep.

THOMAS CHATTERTON
1752–1770

241   *'If wishing for the mystic joys of love'*

If wishing for the mystic joys of love
Is by eternal justice deemed a fault,
Tell me, ye Powers, what woman's innocent.
O how extensive is the power of God!
Conceived in sin, we sin by God's decree
And for such forced iniquity are damned,
For who can say his nature is his own!
Who formed the mind and who instilled the soul,
Who gave us passions which we must obey
But the eternal justice of the God?
And for such forced iniquity we're damned.

GEORGE CRABBE
1754–1832

242   *My Birthday*

Through a dull tract of woe, of dread,
The toiling year has passed and fled:
And, lo! in sad and pensive strain
I sing my birthday date again.

Trembling and poor, I saw the light,
New waking from unconscious night:
Trembling and poor, I still remain
To meet unconscious night again.

Time in my pathway strews few flowers
To cheer or cheat the weary hours;
And those few strangers, dear indeed,
Are choked, are checked, by many a weed.

WILLIAM BLAKE
1757–1827

243   *'The Angel that presided'*

The Angel that presided o'er my birth
Said, 'Little creature, formed of joy and mirth,
Go love without the help of any thing on earth.'

244   *Infant Joy*

I have no name.
I am but two days old.
What shall I call thee?
I happy am,
Joy is my name.
Sweet joy befall thee!

Pretty Joy!
Sweet Joy but two days old.
Sweet Joy I call thee!
Thou dost smile,
I sing the while.
Sweet joy befall thee!

245   *Infant Sorrow*

My mother groaned, my father wept.
Into the dangerous world I leapt:
Helpless, naked, piping loud,
Like a fiend hid in a cloud.

Struggling in my father's hands,
Striving against my swaddling bands,
Bound and weary, I thought best
To sulk upon my mother's breast.

246   *The Clod and the Pebble*

'Love seeketh not itself to please,
Nor for itself hath any care,
But for another gives its ease,
And builds a Heaven in Hell's despair.'

So sang a little clod of clay
Trodden with the cattle's feet;
But a pebble of the brook
Warbled out these metres meet:

'Love seeketh only Self to please,
To bind another to its delight:
Joys in another's loss of ease,
And builds a Hell in Heaven's despite.'

247   *The Sick Rose*

O Rose, thou art sick!
The invisible worm
That flies in the night
In the howling storm

Has found out thy bed
Of crimson joy,
And his dark secret love
Does thy life destroy.

248   *Eternity*

He who binds to himself a joy
Does the wingèd life destroy;
But he who kisses the joy as it flies
Lives in eternity's sunrise.

249 ### *'Mock on, mock on'*

Mock on, mock on, Voltaire, Rousseau;
Mock on, mock on, 'tis all in vain:
You throw the sand against the wind
And the wind blows it back again.

And every sand becomes a gem
Reflected in the beams divine;
Blown back they blind the mocking eye,
But still in Israel's paths they shine.

The atoms of Democritus
And Newton's particles of light
Are sands upon the Red Sea shore
Where Israel's tents do shine so bright.

250 ### *'An old maid early'*

An old maid early—e'er I knew
Aught but the love that on me grew;
And now I'm covered o'er and o'er
And wish that I had been a whore.

O I cannot, cannot find
The undaunted courage of a virgin mind:
For early I in love was crossed,
Before my flower of love was lost.

251 ### *The Question Answered*

What is it men in women do require?
The lineaments of gratified desire.
What is it women do in men require?
The lineaments of gratified desire.

252   *'Great things are done'*

Great things are done when men and mountains meet;
This is not done by jostling in the street.

253   *To the Accuser Who Is the God*
                    of This World

Truly my Satan thou art but a dunce
And dost not know the garment from the man.
Every harlot was a virgin once,
Nor canst thou ever change Kate into Nan.

Though thou art worshipped by the names divine
Of Jesus and Jehovah, thou art still
The Son of Morn in weary night's decline,
The lost traveller's dream under the hill.

ROBERT BURNS
1759–1796

254   *Grace at Kirkudbright*

Some have meat and cannot eat,
Some cannot eat that want it:
But we have meat and we can eat,
Sae let the Lord be thankit.

255   *'Twa bonny lads'*

Twa bonny lads were Sandy and Jockie;
Jockie was loved but Sandy unlucky;
Jockie was laird baith of hills and of valleys,
But Sandy was nought but the king o' gude fellows.

Jockie loved Madgie, for Madgie had money,
And Sandy loved Mary, for Mary was bonny;
Ane wedded for love, ane wedded for treasure,
So Jockie had siller, and Sandy had pleasure.

256 *On a Dog of Lord Eglinton's*

I never barked when out of season,
I never bit without a reason;
I ne'er insulted weaker brother,
Nor wronged by force or fraud another.
We brutes are placed a rank below:
Happy for man could he say so.

MARY LAMB with CHARLES LAMB
1765–1847   1775–1834

257 *Parental Recollections*

A child's a plaything for an hour;
    Its pretty tricks we try
For that or for a longer space;
    Then tire, and lay it by.

But I knew one that to itself
    All seasons could control;
That would have mocked the sense of pain
    Out of a grievèd soul.

Thou straggler into loving arms,
    Young climber up of knees,
When I forget thy thousand ways,
    Then life and all shall cease.

255 siller] silver

ANONYMOUS

?–19th century

258   'Says Tweed to Till'

Says Tweed to Till:
'What gars ye rin sae still?'

Says Till to Tweed:
'Though ye rin with speed
And I rin slaw,
For ae man that ye droon
I droon twa.'

259   'Oh, England!'

Oh, England!
Sick in head and sick in heart,
Sick in whole and every part:
And yet sicker thou art still
For thinking that thou art not ill.

260   'As I walked by my self'

As I walked by my self
And talked to my self,
My self said unto me,
'Look to thy self,
Take care of thy self,
For nobody cares for thee.'

I answered my self,
And said to my self,
In the self-same repartee,
'Look to thy self
Or not look to thy self,
The self-same thing will be.'

258 l. 2] 'Why do you run so slowly?'   ae] each

III

261   *'I saw a peacock'*

I saw a peacock with a fiery tail
I saw a blazing comet drop down hail
I saw a cloud with ivy circled round
I saw a sturdy oak creep on the ground
I saw a pismire swallow up a whale
I saw the raging sea brim full of ale
I saw a Venice glass sixteen foot deep
I saw a well full of men's tears that weep
I saw their eyes all in a flame of fire
I saw a house as big as the moon and higher
I saw the sun even in the midst of night
I saw the man that saw this wondrous sight.

262   *'How many miles to Babylon?'*

How many miles to Babylon?
Three score miles and ten.
Can I get there by candle-light?
Yes, and back again.

If your heels are nimble and light,
You may get there by candle-light.

263   *'My mother said'*

My mother said that I never should
Play with the gypsies in the wood;
The wood was dark, the grass was green,
In came Sally with her tambourine.

I went to the sea—no ship to get across;
I paid ten shillings for a blind white horse;
I up on his back and was off in a crack,
Sally tell my mother I shall never come back.

261 pismire] ant

WILLIAM WORDSWORTH
1770–1850

264   *'She dwelt among the untrodden ways'*

> She dwelt among the untrodden ways
>   Beside the springs of Dove,
> A Maid whom there were none to praise
>   And very few to love:
>
> A violet by a mossy stone
>   Half hidden from the eye!
> —Fair as a star, when only one
>   Is shining in the sky.
>
> She lived unknown, and few could know
>   When Lucy ceased to be;
> But she is in her grave, and, oh,
>   The difference to me!

265   *'My heart leaps up'*

> My heart leaps up when I behold
>   A rainbow in the sky:
> So was it when my life began;
> So is it now I am a man;
> So be it when I shall grow old,
>   Or let me die!
> The Child is father of the Man;
> And I could wish my days to be
> Bound each to each by natural piety.

266   *To a Child*

Written in Her Album

> Small service is true service while it lasts:
> Of humblest friends, bright creature! scorn not one;
> The daisy, by the shadow that it casts,
> Protects the lingering dew-drop from the sun.

SIR WALTER SCOTT

1771–1832

267   *'Look not thou'*

Look not thou on beauty's charming,
Sit thou still when kings are arming,
Taste not when the wine-cup glistens,
Speak not when the people listens,
Stop thine ear against the singer,
From the red gold keep thy finger;
Vacant heart and hand and eye,
Easy live and quiet die.

268   *'Youth! thou wear'st to manhood now'*

Youth! thou wear'st to manhood now
Darker lip and darker brow;
Statelier step, more pensive mien,
In thy face and gait are seen;
Thou must now brook midnight watches,
Take thy food and sport by snatches!
For the gambol and the jest
Thou wert wont to love the best,
Graver follies must thou follow,
But as senseless, false, and hollow.

SAMUEL TAYLOR COLERIDGE
1772–1834

269   *A Sunset*

Upon the mountain's edge with light touch resting,
There a brief while the globe of splendour sits
     And seems a creature of the earth; but soon
       More changeful than the Moon,
To wane fantastic his great orb submits,
Or cone or mow of fire: till sinking slowly
Even to a star at length he lessens wholly.

Abrupt, as Spirits vanish, he is sunk!
A soul-like breeze possesses all the wood.
     The boughs, the sprays, have stood
As motionless as stands the ancient trunk!
But every leaf through all the forest flutters,
And deep the cavern of the fountain mutters.

270   *Time, Real and Imaginary*

An Allegory

On the wide level of a mountain's head,
    (I knew not where, but 'twas some faery place),
Their pinions, ostrich-like, for sails outspread,
Two lovely children run an endless race,
     A sister and a brother!
     This far outstripped the other;
Yet ever runs she with reverted face,
And looks and listens for the boy behind:
     For he, alas! is blind!
O'er rough and smooth with even step he passed,
And knows not whether he be first or last.

269 mow] mound

271   # Apologia Pro Vita Sua

The poet in his lone yet genial hour
Gives to his eyes a magnifying power:
Or rather he emancipates his eyes
From the black shapeless accidents of size—
In unctuous cones of kindling coal,
Or smoke upwreathing from the pipe's trim bowl,
  His gifted ken can see
  Phantoms of sublimity.

272   # *Phantom*

All look and likeness caught from earth,
All accident of kin and birth,
Had passed away. There was no trace
Of aught on that illumined face
Upraised beneath the rifted stone
But of one spirit all her own;—
She, she herself, and only she,
Shone through her body visibly.

273   # *On Imitation*

All are not born to soar—and ah! how few
In tracks where Wisdom leads their paths pursue!
Contagious when to wit or wealth allied
Folly and Vice diffuse their venom wide.
On Folly every fool his talent tries;
It asks some toil to imitate the wise;
Though few like Fox can speak—like Pitt can think—
Yet all like Fox can game—like Pitt can drink.

271 title] A Defence of His Life

ROBERT SOUTHEY
1774–1843

274

The Soldier's Wife
Dactylics

Weary way-wanderer, languid and sick at heart,
Travelling painfully over the rugged road,
Wild-visaged Wanderer! God help thee wretched one!

Sorely thy little one drags by thee bare-footed,
Cold is the baby that hangs at thy bending back,
Meagre and livid and screaming for misery.

Woe-begone mother, half anger, half agony,
As over thy shoulder thou lookest to hush the babe,
Bleakly the blinding snow beats in thy haggèd face.

Ne'er will thy husband return from the war again,
Cold is thy heart and as frozen as Charity!
Cold are thy children.—Now God be thy comforter!

WALTER SAVAGE LANDOR
1775–1864

275

'Had we two met'

Had we two met, blithe-hearted Burns,
   Tho' water is my daily drink,
   May God forgive me but I think
We should have roared our toasts by turns.

Inquisitive low-whispering cares
   Had found no room in either pate,
   Until I asked thee, rather late,
Is there a hand-rail to the stairs?

276 *Dirce*

Stand close around, ye Stygian set,
    With Dirce in one boat conveyed!
Or Charon, seeing, may forget
    That he is old and she a shade.

277 *Plays*

Alas, how soon the hours are over,
Counted us out to play the lover!
And how much narrower is the stage,
Allotted us to play the sage!

But when we play the fool, how wide
The theatre expands! beside,
How long the audience sits before us!
How many prompters! what a chorus!

278 *'Ireland never was contented'*

Ireland never was contented.
Say you so? You are demented.
Ireland was contented when
All could use the sword and pen,
And when Tara rose so high
That her turrets split the sky,
And about her courts were seen
Liveried angels robed in green,
Wearing, by St Patrick's bounty,
Emeralds big as half the county.

279 *'Death stands above me'*

Death stands above me, whispering low
    I know not what into my ear;
Of his strange language all I know
    Is, there is not a word of fear.

THOMAS MOORE
1779–1852

280   *Venetian Air*

Row gently here, my gondolier; so softly wake the tide,
That not an ear on earth may hear, but hers to whom we glide.
Had Heaven but tongues to speak, as well as starry eyes to see,
Oh! think what tales 'twould have to tell of wandering youths
    like me!

Now rest thee here, my gondolier; hush, hush, for up I go,
To climb yon light balcòny's height, while thou keep'st watch
    below.
Ah! did we take for Heaven above but half such pains as we
Take day and night for woman's love, what angels we should
    be!

281   *An Argument*

To Any Phillis or Chloe

I've oft been told by learned friars,
    That wishing and the crime are one,
And Heaven punishes desires
    As much as if the deed were done.

If wishing damns us, you and I
    Are damned to all our heart's content;
Come, then, at least we may enjoy
    Some pleasure for our punishment!

282 *Song*

When the heart's feeling
Burns with concealing,
Glances will tell what we fear to confess:
Oh! what an anguish
Silent to languish,
Could we not look all we wish to express!

When half-expiring,
Restless, desiring,
Lovers wish something, but must not say what,
Looks tell the wanting,
Looks tell the granting,
Looks betray all that the heart would be at.

283 *To Miss ——*

With woman's form and woman's tricks
So much of man you seem to mix,
 One knows not where to take you:
I pray you, if 'tis not too far,
Go, ask of Nature *which* you are,
 Or what she meant to make you.

Yet stay—you need not take the pains—
With neither beauty, youth, nor brains
 For man or maid's desiring;
Pert as female, fool as male,
As boy too green, as girl too stale—
 The thing's not worth inquiring!

284 *To —— ——*

When I loved you, I can't but allow
 I had many an exquisite minute;
But the scorn that I feel for you now
 Hath even more luxury in it!

Thus, whether we're on or we're off,
  Some witchery seems to await you;
To love you is pleasant enough,
  And, oh! 'tis delicious to hate you!

THOMAS LOVE PEACOCK
1785–1866

285   *Beneath the Cypress Shade*

I dug, beneath the cypress shade,
  What well might seem an elfin's grave;
And every pledge in earth I laid,
  That erst thy false affection gave.

I pressed them down the sod beneath;
  I placed one mossy stone above;
And twined the rose's fading wreath
  Around the sepulchre of love.

Frail as thy love, the flowers were dead,
  Ere yet the evening sun was set:
But years shall see the cypress spread,
  Immutable as my regret.

GEORGE GORDON, LORD BYRON
1788–1824

286   *'So we'll go no more a-roving'*

So we'll go no more a-roving
  So late into the night,
Though the heart be still as loving
  And the moon be still as bright.

For the sword outwears its sheath,
    And the soul wears out the breast,
And the heart must pause to breathe,
    And Love itself have rest.

Though the night was made for loving,
    And the day returns too soon,
Yet we'll go no more a-roving
    By the light of the moon.

287   *'I would to Heaven'*

I would to Heaven that I were so much clay,
    As I am blood, bone, marrow, passion, feeling—
Because at least the past were passed away,
    And for the future—(but I write this reeling,
Having got drunk exceedingly today,
    So that I seem to stand upon the ceiling)
I say—the future is a serious matter—
And so—for God's sake—hock and soda-water!

288   *'Remember thee! remember thee!'*

Remember thee! remember thee!
    Till Lethe quench Life's burning stream
Remorse and Shame shall cling to thee,
    And haunt thee like a feverish dream!

Remember thee! Aye, doubt it not.
    Thy husband too shall think of thee:
By neither shalt thou be forgot,
    Thou *false* to him, thou *fiend* to me!

289   *Lines Written Beneath a Picture*

Dear object of defeated care!
    Though now of Love and thee bereft,
To reconcile me with despair
    Thine image and my tears are left.

'Tis said with Sorrow Time can cope;
   But this I feel can ne'er be true:
For by the death-blow of my Hope
   My Memory immortal grew.

290   *Answer to ——'s Professions of Affection*

In hearts like thine ne'er may I hold a place
Till I renounce all sense, all shame, all grace—
That seat—like seats, the bane of Freedom's realm,
But dear to those presiding at the helm—
Is basely purchased, not with gold alone;
Add Conscience, too, this bargain is your own—
'Tis thine to offer with corrupting art
The *rotten borough* of the human heart.

291   *'They say that Hope is happiness'*

They say that Hope is happiness;
   But genuine Love must prize the past,
And Memory wakes the thoughts that bless:
   They rose the first—they set the last;

And all that Memory loves the most
   Was once our only Hope to be,
And all that Hope adored and lost
   Hath melted into Memory.

Alas! it is delusion all;
   The future cheats us from afar,
Nor can we be what we recall,
   Nor dare we think on what we are.

PERCY BYSSHE SHELLEY

1792–1822

292   *A Song*

A widow bird sate mourning for her love
  Upon a wintry bough;
The frozen wind crept on above,
  The freezing stream below.

There was no leaf upon the forest bare,
  No flower upon the ground,
And little motion in the air
  Except the mill-wheel's sound.

293   *The Waning Moon*

And like a dying lady, lean and pale,
Who totters forth, wrapped in a gauzy veil,
Out of her chamber, led by the insane
And feeble wanderings of her fading brain,
The moon arose up in the murky East,
A white and shapeless mass.

294   *Lines to a Reviewer*

Alas, good friend, what profit can you see
In hating such a hateless thing as me?
There is no sport in hate where all the rage
Is on one side: in vain would you assuage
Your frowns upon an unresisting smile,
In which not even contempt lurks to beguile
Your heart, by some faint sympathy of hate.
Oh, conquer what you cannot satiate!
For to your passion I am far more coy
Than ever yet was coldest maid or boy
In winter noon. Of your antipathy
If I am the Narcissus, you are free
To pine into a sound with hating me.

295

To ——

Music, when soft voices die,
Vibrates in the memory—
Odours, when sweet violets sicken,
Live within the sense they quicken.

Rose leaves, when the rose is dead,
Are heaped for the beloved's bed;
And so thy thoughts, when thou art gone,
Love itself shall slumber on.

JOHN CLARE
1793–1864

296

Field Path

The beans in blossom with their spots of jet
Smelt sweet as gardens wheresoever met;
The level meadow grass was in the swath;
The hedge briar rose hung right across the path,
White over with its flowers—the grass that lay
Bleaching beneath the twittering heat to hay
Smelt so deliciously, the puzzled bee
Went wondering where the honeyed sweets could be;
And passer-by along the level rows
Stooped down and whipt a bit beneath his nose.

297 *Lines Written on a Very Boisterous Day
in May, 1844*

'Tis May, and yet the skies are overcast
    With clouds resembling a rough storm at sea,
'Tis May, and yet the hurricane goes past
    In dust, like foaming billows o'er the lea
    High overhead, close by me, and 'tis He
Who walks the sea, and drives the ships away
    From anchor into wrecks! Here I am free
From danger, and the fields and woods the bay
To rest my weary limbs amid the storms of May.

298 *Solitude*

There is a charm in solitude that cheers,
A feeling that the world knows nothing of;
A green delight the wounded mind endears
After the hustling world is broken off,
Whose whole delight was crime—at good to scoff.
Green solitude, his prison, pleasure yields,
The bitch fox heeds him not; birds seem to laugh.
He lives the Crusoe of his lonely field
Whose dark green oaks his noontide leisure shield.

299 *Fragment*

Language has not the power to speak what love indites:
The Soul lies buried in the ink that writes.

300 *Birds' Nests*

'Tis spring, warm glows the south,
Chaffinch carries the moss in his mouth
To filbert hedges all day long,
And charms the poet with his beautiful song;
The wind blows bleak o'er the sedgy fen,
But warm the sun shines by the little wood,
Where the old cow at her leisure chews her cud.

JOHN KEATS
1795–1821

301   *'This living hand'*

This living hand, now warm and capable
Of earnest grasping, would, if it were cold
And in the icy silence of the tomb,
So haunt thy days and chill thy dreaming nights
That thou wouldst wish thine own heart dry of blood
So in my veins red life might stream again,
And thou be conscience-calmed—see here it is—
I hold it towards you.

THOMAS LOVELL BEDDOES
1803–1849

302   *Song*

from *The Second Brother*

Strew not earth with empty stars,
    Strew it not with roses,
Nor feathers from the crest of Mars,
Nor summer's idle posies.
'Tis not the primrose-sandalled moon,
    Nor cold and silent morn,
Nor he that climbs the dusty noon,
Nor mower war with scythe that drops,
Stuck with helmed and turbaned tops
    Of enemies new-shorn.
Ye cups, ye lyres, ye trumpets know,
Pour your music, let it flow,
'Tis Bacchus' son who walks below.

RALPH WALDO EMERSON
1803–1882

303   *Letters*

Every day brings a ship,
Every ship brings a word;
Well for those who have no fear,
Looking seaward, well assured
That the word the vessel brings
Is the word they wish to hear.

304   *Days*

Daughters of Time, the hypocritic Days,
Muffled and dumb like barefoot dervishes,
And marching single in an endless file,
Bring diadems and faggots in their hands.
To each they offer gifts after his will,
Bread, kingdoms, stars, and sky that holds them all.
I, in my pleached garden, watched the pomp,
Forgot my morning wishes, hastily
Took a few herbs and apples, and the Day
Turned and departed silent. I, too late,
Under her solemn fillet saw the scorn.

305   *Character*

The sun set, but set not his hope:
Stars rose; his faith was earlier up:
Fixed on the enormous galaxy,
Deeper and older seemed his eye;
And matched his sufferance sublime
The taciturnity of time.
He spoke, and words more soft than rain
Brought the Age of Gold again:
His action won such reverence sweet
As hid all measure of the feat.

306   *Quatrain: Poet*

To clothe the fiery thought
In simple words succeeds,
For still the craft of genius is
To mask a king in weeds.

307   *Water*

The water understands
Civilization well;
It wets my foot, but prettily,
It chills my life, but wittily,
It is not disconcerted,
It is not broken-hearted:
Well used, it decketh joy,
Adorneth, doubleth joy:
Ill used, it will destroy,
In perfect time and measure
With a face of golden pleasure
Elegantly destroy.

308   *Limits*

Who knows this or that?
Hark in the wall to the rat:
Since the world was, he has gnawed;
Of his wisdom, of his fraud
What dost thou know?
In the wretched little beast
Is life and heart,
Child and parent,
Not without relation
To fruitful field and sun and moon.
What art thou? His wicked eye
Is cruel to thy cruelty.

ELIZABETH BARRETT BROWNING
1806–1861

309 *The Best*

What's the best thing in the world?
June-rose, by May-dew impearl'd;
Sweet south-wind, that means no rain;
Truth, not cruel to a friend;
Pleasure, not in haste to end;
Beauty, not self-deck'd and curl'd
Till its pride is over-plain;
Light, that never makes you wink;
Memory, that gives no pain;
Love, when, *so*, you're loved again.
What's the best thing in the world?
—Something out of it, I think.

JOHN GREENLEAF WHITTIER
1807–1892

310 *All's Well*

The clouds, which rise with thunder, slake
    Our thirsty souls with rain;
The blow most dreaded falls to break
    From off our limbs a chain;
And wrongs of man to man but make
    The love of God more plain.
As through the shadowy lens of even
The eye looks farthest into heaven
On gleams of star and depths of blue
The glaring sunshine never knew!

ALFRED, LORD TENNYSON
1809–1892

311   *'From sorrow sorrow yet is born'*

From sorrow sorrow yet is born,
  Hopes flow like water through a sieve,
But leave not thou thy son forlorn;
  Touch me, great Nature, make me live.

As when thy sunlights, a mild heat,
  Touch some dun mere that sleepeth still;
As when thy moonlights, dim and sweet,
  Touch some gray ruin on the hill.

312   *The Eagle*

He clasps the crag with crooked hands;
Close to the sun in lonely lands,
Ringed with the azure world, he stands.

The wrinkled sea beneath him crawls;
He watches from his mountain walls,
And like a thunderbolt he falls.

313   *A Dedication*

Dear, near and true—no truer Time himself
Can prove you, though he make you evermore
Dearer and nearer, as the rapid of life
Shoots to the fall—take this and pray that he
Who wrote it, honouring your sweet faith in him,
May trust himself; and after praise and scorn,
As one who feels the immeasurable world,
Attain the wise indifference of the wise;
And after Autumn past—if left to pass
His autumn into seeming-leafless days—
Draw toward the long frost and longest night,
Wearing his wisdom lightly, like the fruit
Which in our winter woodland looks a flower.

314   *'I stood on a tower in the wet'*

I stood on a tower in the wet,
And New Year and Old Year met,
And winds were roaring and blowing;
And I said, 'O years, that meet in tears,
Have ye aught that is worth the knowing?
Science enough and exploring,
Wanderers coming and going,
Matter enough for deploring,
But aught that is worth the knowing?'
Seas at my feet were flowing,
Waves on the shingle pouring,
Old Year roaring and blowing,
And New Year blowing and roaring.

315   *'Somebody being a nobody'*

Somebody being a nobody,
Thinking to look like a somebody,
Said that he thought me a nobody:
Good little somebody-nobody,
Had you not known me a somebody,
Would you have called me a nobody?

316   Frater Ave atque Vale

Row us out from Desenzano, to your Sirmione row!
So they rowed, and there we landed—'O venusta Sirmio!'
There to me through all the groves of olive in the summer glow,
There beneath the Roman ruin where the purple flowers grow,
Came that 'Ave atque Vale' of the Poet's hopeless woe,
Tenderest of all Roman poets nineteen-hundred years ago,
'Frater Ave atque Vale'—as we wandered to and fro
Gazing at the Lydian laughter of the Garda Lake below
Sweet Catullus's all-but-island, olive-silvery Sirmio!

316 title] Brother, Hail and Farewell   l.2] 'O lovely Sirmio!'

ROBERT BROWNING
1812–1889

317   *Home Thoughts from the Sea*

Nobly, nobly Cape Saint Vincent to the north-west died away;
Sunset ran, one glorious blood-red, reeking into Cádiz bay;
Bluish mid the burning water, full in face Trafalgar lay;
In the dimmest north-east distance, dawned Gibraltar grand
    and gray;
'Here and here did England help me,—how can I help
    England?'—say,
Whoso turns as I, this evening, turn to God to praise and pray,
While Jove's planet rises yonder, silent over Africa.

318   *Meeting at Night*

    The grey sea and the long black land;
    And the yellow half-moon large and low;
    And the startled little waves that leap
    In fiery ringlets from their sleep,
    As I gain the cove with pushing prow,
    And quench its speed in the slushy sand.

    Then a mile of warm sea-scented beach;
    Three fields to cross till a farm appears;
    A tap at the pane, the quick sharp scratch
    And blue spurt of a lighted match,
    And a voice less loud, through its joys and fears,
    Than the two hearts beating each to each!

319   *Parting at Morning*

    Round the cape of a sudden came the sea,
    And the sun looked over the mountain's rim—
    And straight was a path of gold for him,
    And the need of a world of men for me.

133

320 *Among the Rocks*

from *James Lee's Wife*

Oh, good gigantic smile o' the brown old earth,
   This autumn morning! How he sets his bones
To bask i' the sun, and thrusts out knees and feet
For the ripple to run over in its mirth;
   Listening the while, where on the heap of stones
The white breast of the sea-lark twitters sweet.

That is the doctrine, simple, ancient, true;
   Such is life's trial, as old earth smiles and knows.
If you loved only what were worth your love,
Love were clear gain, and wholly well for you:
   Make the low nature better by your throes!
Give earth yourself, go up for gain above!

321 *'When I vexed you'*

from *Ferishtah's Fancies*

When I vexed you, and you chid me,
   And I owned my fault and turned
My cheek the way you bid me,
   And confessed the blow well earned,—

My comfort all the while was
   —Fault was faulty—near, not quite!
Do you wonder why the smile was?
   O'erpunished wrong grew right.

But faults you ne'er suspected,
   Nay, praised, no faults at all,—
Those would you had detected—
   Crushed eggs whence snakes could crawl!

ROBERT BROWNING

322 *To Edward FitzGerald*

I chanced upon a new book yesterday:
I opened it, and where my finger lay
  'Twixt page and uncut page these words I read
—Some six or seven at most—and learned thereby
That you, FitzGerald, whom by ear and eye
  She never knew, 'thanked God my wife was dead'.

Ay, dead! and were yourself alive, good Fitz,
How to return you thanks would task my wits:
  Kicking you seems the common lot of curs—
While more appropriate greeting lends you grace:
Surely to spit there glorifies your face—
  Spitting—from lips once sanctified by Hers.

323 *Appearances*

And so you found that poor room dull,
  Dark, hardly to your taste, my dear?
Its features seemed unbeautiful:
  But this I know—'twas there, not here,
You plighted troth to me, the word
Which—ask that poor room how it heard!

And this rich room obtains your praise
  Unqualified,—so bright, so fair,
So all whereat perfection stays?
  Ay, but remember—here, not there,
The other word was spoken!—Ask
This rich room how you dropped the mask!

324 *Bad Dreams*

Last night I saw you in my sleep:
  And how your charm of face was changed!
I asked, 'Some love, some faith you keep?'
  You answered, 'Faith gone, love estranged.'

ROBERT BROWNING

Whereat I woke—a twofold bliss:
    Waking was one, but next there came
This other: 'Though I felt, for this,
    My heart break, I loved on the same.'

HENRY THOREAU
1817–1862

325   *'Light-winged Smoke, Icarian bird'*

Light-winged Smoke, Icarian bird,
Melting thy pinions in thy upward flight,
Lark without song, and messenger of dawn,
Circling above the hamlets as they nest;
Or else, departing dream, and shadowy form
Of midnight vision, gathering up thy skirts;
By night star-veiling, and by day
Darkening the light and blotting out the sun;
Go thou my incense upward from this hearth,
And ask the gods to pardon this clear flame.

326   *'Each more melodious note I hear'*

    Each more melodious note I hear
    Brings this reproach to me,
    That I alone afford the ear,
    Who would the music be.

327 *On the Sun Coming Out in the Afternoon*

Methinks all things have travelled since you shined,
But only Time, and clouds, Time's team, have moved;
Again foul weather shall not change my mind,
But in the shade I will believe what in the sun I loved.

136

328 *'For though the eaves were rabbeted'*

For though the eaves were rabbeted,
    And the well-sweeps were slanted,
Each house seemed not inhabited
    But haunted.

The pensive traveller held his way,
    Silent and melancholy,
For every man an idiot was,
    And every house a folly.

329 *'They made me erect and lone'*

They made me erect and lone
And within me is the bone
Where I sit there is my throne.
If ye choose to sit apart
If ye choose give me the start
Take the sap and leave the heart.
Still my vision will be clear
Still my life will not be drear:
To the center all is near.

EMILY BRONTË
1818–1848

330 *Fall, leaves, fall*

Fall, leaves, fall; die, flowers, away;
Lengthen night and shorten day;
Every leaf speaks bliss to me
Fluttering from the autumn tree.
I shall smile when wreaths of snow
Blossom where the rose should grow;
I shall sing when night's decay
Ushers in a drearier day.

328 rabbeted] grooved for carpentry joints   well-sweeps] balanced poles for raising
water; slanted in use

ARTHUR HUGH CLOUGH
1819–1861

331   *Darkness*

But that from slow dissolving pomps of dawn
No verity of slowly strengthening light
Early or late hath issued; that the day
Scarce-shown, relapses rather, self-withdrawn,
Back to the glooms of ante-natal night,
For this, O human beings, mourn we may.

332   *'To spend uncounted years of pain'*

To spend uncounted years of pain,
Again, again, and yet again,
In working out in heart and brain
    The problem of our being here;
To gather facts from far and near,
Upon the mind to hold them clear,
And, knowing more may yet appear,
Unto one's latest breath to fear
The premature result to draw—
Is this the object, end, and law,
    And purpose of our being here?

JAMES RUSSELL LOWELL
1819–1891

333   *Sixty-Eighth Birthday*

As life runs on, the road grows strange
With faces new, and near the end
The milestones into headstones change,
'Neath every one a friend.

HERMAN MELVILLE
1819–1891

334   *Monody*

To have known him, to have loved him
   After loneness long;
And then to be estranged in life,
   And neither in the wrong;
And now for death to set his seal—
   Ease me, a little ease, my song!

By wintry hills his hermit-mound
   The sheeted snow-drifts drape,
And houseless there the snow-bird flits
   Beneath the fir-trees' crape:
Glazed now with ice the cloistral vine
   That hid the shyest grape.

335   *Fragments of a Lost Gnostic Poem*
            of the Twelfth Century

I

Found a family, build a state,
The pledged event is still the same:
Matter in end will never abate
His ancient brutal claim.

II

Indolence is heaven's ally here,
And energy the child of hell:
The Good Man pouring from his pitcher clear
But brims the poisoned well.

336 *In the Pauper's Turnip-Field*

Crow, in pulpit lone and tall
Of yon charred hemlock, grimly dead,
Why on me in preachment call—
Me, by nearer preachment led
Here in homily of my hoe.
The hoe, the hoe,
My heavy hoe
That earthward bows me to foreshow
A mattock heavier than the hoe.

WALT WHITMAN
1819–1892

337 *Are You the New Person Drawn Toward Me?*

Are you the new person drawn toward me?
To begin with take warning, I am surely far different from what
you suppose;
Do you suppose you will find in me your ideal?
Do you think it is so easy to have me become your lover?
Do you think the friendship of me would be unalloy'd
satisfaction?
Do you think I am trusty and faithful?
Do you see no further than this façade, this smooth and tolerant
manner of me?
Do you suppose yourself advancing on real ground toward a real
heroic man?
Have you no thought O dreamer that it may be all maya,
illusion?

338 *Sometimes With One I Love*

Sometimes with one I love I fill myself with rage for fear I
effuse unreturn'd love,
But now I think there is no unreturn'd love, the pay is certain
one way or another,
(I loved a certain person ardently and my love was not return'd,
Yet out of that I have written these songs).

339 *Reconciliation*

Word over all, beautiful as the sky,
Beautiful that war and all its deeds of carnage must in time be
    utterly lost,
That the hands of the sisters Death and Night incessantly softly
    wash again, and ever again, this soil'd world;
For my enemy is dead, a man divine as myself is dead,
I look where he lies white-faced and still in the coffin—I draw
    near,
Bend down and touch lightly with my lips the white face in the
    coffin.

340 *A Noiseless Patient Spider*

A noiseless patient spider,
I mark'd where on a little promontory it stood isolated,
Mark'd how to explore the vacant vast surrounding,
It launch'd forth filament, filament, filament, out of itself,
Ever unreeling them, ever tirelessly speeding them.

And you O my soul where you stand,
Surrounded, detached, in measureless oceans of space,
Ceaselessly musing, venturing, throwing, seeking the spheres to
    connect them,
Till the bridge you will need be form'd, till the ductile anchor
    hold,
Till the gossamer thread you fling catch somewhere, O my soul.

341 *The Last Invocation*

At the last, tenderly,
From the walls of the powerful fortress'd house,
From the clasp of the knitted locks, from the keep of the well-
    closed doors,
Let me be wafted.

Let me glide noiselessly forth;
With the key of softness unlock the locks—with a whisper,
Set ope the doors O soul.

Tenderly—be not impatient,
(Strong is your hold O mortal flesh,
Strong is your hold O love).

342 *Ah Poverties, Wincings, and Sulky Retreats*

Ah poverties, wincings, and sulky retreats,
Ah you foes that in conflict have overcome me,
(For what is my life or any man's life but a conflict with foes,
    the old, the incessant war?)
You degradations, you tussle with passions and appetites,
You smarts from dissatisfied friendships, (ah wounds the
    sharpest of all!)
You toil of painful and choked articulations, you meannesses,
You shallow tongue-talks at tables, (my tongue the shallowest of
    any;)
You broken resolutions, you racking angers, you smother'd
    ennuis!
Ah think not you finally triumph, my real self has yet to come
    forth,
It shall yet march forth o'ermastering, till all lies beneath me,
It shall yet stand up the soldier of ultimate victory.

343   *Old War-Dreams*

In midnight sleep of many a face of anguish,
Of the look at first of the mortally wounded, (of that
    indescribable look,)
Of the dead on their backs with arms extended wide,
    I dream, I dream, I dream.

Of scenes of Nature, fields and mountains,
Of skies so beauteous after a storm, and at night the moon so
    unearthly bright,
Shining sweetly, shining down, where we dig the trenches and
    gather the heaps,
    I dream, I dream, I dream.

Long have they pass'd, faces and trenches and fields,
Where through the carnage I moved with a callous composure,
    or away from the fallen,
Onward I sped at the time—but now of their forms at night,
  I dream, I dream, I dream.

344   *A Clear Midnight*

This is thy hour O Soul, thy free flight into the wordless,
Away from books, away from art, the day erased, the lesson
  done,
Thee fully forth emerging, silent, gazing, pondering the themes
  thou lovest best,
Night, sleep, death and the stars.

345   *To the Pending Year*

Have I no weapon-word for thee—some message brief and
  fierce?
(Have I fought out and done indeed the battle?) Is there no shot
  left,
For all thy affectations, lisps, scorns, manifold silliness?
Nor for myself—my own rebellious self in thee?

Down, down, proud gorge!—though choking thee;
Thy bearded throat and high-borne forehead to the gutter;
Crouch low thy neck to eleemosynary gifts.

MATTHEW ARNOLD
1822–1888

346   *Destiny*

    Why each is striving, from of old,
    To love more deeply than he can?
    Still would be true, yet still grows cold?
    —Ask of the Powers that sport with man!

They yoked in him, for endless strife,
A heart of ice, a soul of fire;
And hurled him on the Field of Life,
An aimless unallayed Desire.

347   *'Below the surface-stream'*

Below the surface-stream, shallow and light,
Of what we *say* we feel—below the stream,
As light, of what we *think* we feel—there flows
With noiseless current strong, obscure and deep,
The central stream of what we feel indeed.

WILLIAM CORY
1823–1892

348   *Heraclitus*

They told me, Heraclitus, they told me you were dead,
They brought me bitter news to hear and bitter tears to shed.
I wept as I remember'd how often you and I
Had tired the sun with talking and sent him down the sky.

And now that thou art lying, my dear old Carian guest,
A handful of grey ashes, long, long ago at rest,
Still are thy pleasant voices, thy nightingales, awake;
For Death, he taketh all away, but them he cannot take.

WILLIAM ALLINGHAM
1824–1889

349   *A Mill*

Two leaps the water from its race
  Made to the brook below;
The first leap it was curving glass,
  The second bounding snow.

COVENTRY PATMORE
1825–1896

350   *The Revelation*

An idle poet, here and there,
   Looks round him; but, for all the rest,
The world, unfathomably fair,
   Is duller than a witling's jest.
Love wakes men, once a lifetime each;
   They lift their heavy lids, and look;
And lo, what one sweet page can teach,
   They read with joy, then shut the book.
And some give thanks, and some blaspheme,
   And most forget; but, either way,
That and the Child's unheeded dream
   Is all the light of all their day.

351   *The Spirit's Epochs*

Not in the crises of events,
   Of compass'd hopes, or fears fulfill'd,
Or acts of gravest consequence,
   Are life's delight and depth reveal'd.
The day of days was not the day;
   That went before, or was postponed;
The night Death took our lamp away
   Was not the night on which we groan'd.
I drew my bride, beneath the moon,
   Across my threshold; happy hour!
But, ah, the walk that afternoon
   We saw the water-flags in flower!

352   *Constancy Rewarded*

I vow'd unvarying faith; and she,
   To whom in full I pay that vow,
Rewards me with variety
   Which men who change can never know.

353 ## Magna Est Veritas

Here, in this little Bay,
Full of tumultuous life and great repose,
Where, twice a day,
The purposeless, glad ocean comes and goes,
Under high cliffs, and far from the huge town,
I sit me down.
For want of me the world's course will not fail:
When all its work is done, the lie shall rot;
The truth is great, and shall prevail,
When none cares whether it prevail or not.

DANTE GABRIEL ROSSETTI
1828–1882

354 ## Aspecta Medusa

Andromeda, by Perseus saved and wed,
Hankered each day to see the Gorgon's head:
Till o'er a fount he held it, bade her lean,
And mirrored in the wave was safely seen
That death she lived by.

Let not thine eyes know
Any forbidden thing itself, although
It once should save as well as kill: but be
Its shadow upon life enough for thee.

355 ## *Memory*

Is Memory most of miseries miserable,
Or the one flower of ease in bitterest hell?

353 title] The Truth is Great
354 title] Medusa Seen

EMILY DICKINSON
1830–1886

356

'*I like a look of agony*'

I like a look of agony,
Because I know it's true;
Men do not sham convulsion,
Nor simulate a throe.

The eyes glaze once, and that is death.
Impossible to feign
The beads upon the forehead
By homely anguish strung.

357

'*I'm Nobody!*'

I'm Nobody! Who are you?
Are you Nobody too?
Then there's a pair of us?
Don't tell! They'd advertise, you know!

How dreary to be Somebody!
How public—like a frog—
To tell one's name the livelong June
To an admiring bog!

358

'*They say that time assuages*'

They say that time assuages.
Time never did assuage.
An actual suffering strengthens,
As sinews do, with age.

Time is a test of trouble
But not a remedy.
If such it prove, it prove too
There was no malady.

359 *'It dropped so low'*

It dropped so low in my regard
I heard it hit the ground
And go to pieces on the stones
At bottom of my mind;

Yet blamed the fate that fractured less
Than I reviled myself
For entertaining plated wares
Upon my silver shelf.

360 *'I stepped from plank to plank'*

I stepped from plank to plank,
A slow and cautious way;
The stars about my head I felt,
About my feet the sea.

I knew not but the next
Would be my final inch.
This gave me that precarious gait
Some call experience.

361 *'The stimulus beyond the grave'*

The stimulus beyond the grave
His countenance to see
Supports me like imperial drams
Afforded day by day.

362 *'We miss a kinsman more'*

We miss a kinsman more
When warranted to see
Than when withheld of oceans
From possibility.

A furlong than a league
Inflicts a pricklier pain,
Till we, who smiled at Pyrenees,
Of parishes complain.

363   *'It sounded as if the streets were running'*

It sounded as if the streets were running,
And then the streets stood still;
Eclipse was all we could see at the window
And awe was all we could feel.

By and by, the boldest stole out of his covert
To see if Time were there.
Nature was in an opal apron,
Mixing fresher air.

364   *'Drowning is not so pitiful'*

Drowning is not so pitiful
As the attempt to rise.
Three times, 'tis said, a sinking man
Comes up to face the skies,
And then declines forever
To that abhorred abode,
Where hope and he part company —
For he is grasped of God.
The Maker's cordial visage,
However good to see,
Is shunned, we must admit it,
Like an adversity.

365   *'My life closed twice before its close'*

My life closed twice before its close.
It yet remains to see
If immortality unveil
A third event to me,

So huge, so hopeless to conceive
As these that twice befell.
Parting is all we know of heaven,
And all we need of hell.

CHRISTINA ROSSETTI
1830–1894

366   *What Would I Give?*

What would I give for a heart of flesh to warm me through,
Instead of this heart of stone ice-cold whatever I do;
Hard and cold and small, of all hearts the worst of all.

What would I give for words, if only words would come;
But now in its misery my spirit has fallen dumb:
Oh, merry friends, go your way, I have never a word to say.

What would I give for tears, not smiles but scalding tears,
To wash the black mark clean, and to thaw the frost of years,
To wash the stain ingrain and to make me clean again.

EDWARD BULWER, EARL OF LYTTON
1831–1891

367   *The Last Wish*

Since all that I can ever do for thee
Is to do nothing, this my prayer must be:
That thou mayst never guess nor ever see
The all-endured this nothing-done costs me.

JOHN WARREN, LORD DE TABLEY
1835–1895

368   *The Power of Interval*

A fair girl tripping out to meet her love,
Trimmed in her best, fresh as a clover bud.
An old crone leaning at an ember'd fire,
Short-breath'd in sighs and moaning to herself—
And all the interval of stealing years
To make that this, and one by one detach
Some excellent condition; till Despair
Faint at the vision, sadly, fiercely blinds
Her burning eyes on her forgetful hands.

THOMAS HARDY
1840–1928

369   *'I Look Into My Glass'*

I look into my glass,
And view my wasting skin,
And say, 'Would God it came to pass
My heart had shrunk as thin!'

For then, I, undistrest
By hearts grown cold to me,
Could lonely wait my endless rest
With equanimity.

But Time, to make me grieve,
Part steals, lets part abide;
And shakes this fragile frame at eve
With throbbings of noontide.

370 ## *A Thunderstorm in Town*

She wore a new 'terra-cotta' dress,
And we stayed, because of the pelting storm,
Within the hansom's dry recess,
Though the horse had stopped; yea, motionless
    We sat on, snug and warm.

Then the downpour ceased, to my sharp sad pain,
And the glass that had screened our forms before
Flew up, and out she sprang to her door:
I should have kissed her if the rain
    Had lasted a minute more.

371 ## *The Peace-Offering*

It was but a little thing,
Yet I knew it meant to me
Ease from what had given a sting
To the very birdsinging
    Latterly.

But I would not welcome it;
And for all I then declined
O the regrettings infinite
When the night-processions flit
    Through the mind!

372 ## *The Pink Frock*

'O my pretty pink frock,
I shan't be able to wear it!
Why is he dying just now?
    I hardly can bear it!

'He might have contrived to live on;
But they say there's no hope whatever:
And must I shut myself up,
    And go out never?

'O my pretty pink frock!
Puff-sleeved and accordion-pleated!
He might have passed in July,
    And not so cheated!'

373   *On Sturminster Foot-Bridge*

                    (Onomatopoeic)

Reticulations creep upon the slack stream's face
    When the wind skims irritably past,
The current clucks smartly into each hollow place
That years of flood have scrabbled in the pier's sodden base:
    The floating-lily leaves rot fast.

On a roof stand the swallows ranged in wistful waiting rows,
    Till they arrow off and drop like stones
Among the eyot-withies at whose foot the river flows:
And beneath the roof is she who in the dark world shows
    As a lattice-gleam when midnight moans.

374   *The Nettles*

        This, then, is the grave of my son,
        Whose heart she won! And nettles grow
    Upon his mound; and she lives just below.

        How he upbraided me, and left,
        And our lives were cleft, because I said
    She was hard, unfeeling, caring but to wed.

        Well, to see this sight I have fared these miles,
        And her firelight smiles from her window there,
    Whom he left his mother to cherish with tender care!

        It is enough. I'll turn and go;
        Yes, nettles grow where lone lies he,
    Who spurned me for seeing what he could not see.

153

THOMAS HARDY

375 *The Fallow Deer at the Lonely House*

One without looks in to-night
  Through the curtain-chink
From the sheet of glistening white;
One without looks in to-night
   As we sit and think
   By the fender-brink.

We do not discern those eyes
   Watching in the snow;
Lit by lamps of rosy dyes
We do not discern those eyes
   Wondering, aglow,
   Fourfooted, tiptoe.

376 *The Lodging-House Fuchsias*

Mrs Masters's fuchsias hung
Higher and broader, and brightly swung,
  Bell-like, more and more
Over the narrow garden-path,
Giving the passer a sprinkle-bath
  In the morning.

She put up with their pushful ways,
And made us tenderly lift their sprays,
  Going to her door:
But when her funeral had to pass
They cut back all the flowery mass
  In the morning.

GERARD MANLEY HOPKINS
1844–1889

377   *Heaven-Haven*
A Nun Takes the Veil

I have desired to go
    Where springs not fail,
To fields where flies no sharp and sided hail
And a few lilies blow.

And I have asked to be
    Where no storms come,
Where the green swell is in the havens dumb,
And out of the swing of the sea.

378   *Pied Beauty*

Glory be to God for dappled things—
   For skies of couple-colour as a brinded cow;
     For rose-moles all in stipple upon trout that swim;
Fresh-firecoal chestnut-falls; finches' wings;
   Landscape plotted and pierced—fold, fallow, and plough;
     And áll trádes, their gear and tackle and trim.

All things counter, original, spare, strange;
   Whatever is fickle, freckled (who knows how?)
     With swift, slow; sweet, sour; adazzle, dim;
He fathers-forth whose beauty is past change:
                  Praise him.

379 *Peace*

When will you ever, Peace, wild wooddove, shy wings shut,
Your round me roaming end, and under be my boughs?
When, when, Peace, will you, Peace?—I'll not play hypocrite

To own my heart: I yield you do come sometimes; but
That piecemeal peace is poor peace. What pure peace allows
Alarms of wars, the daunting wars, the death of it?

O surely, reaving Peace, my Lord should leave in lieu
Some good! And so he does leave Patience exquisite,
That plumes to Peace thereafter. And when Peace here does
    house
He comes with work to do, he does not come to coo,
                                 He comes to brood and sit.

380 *'How looks the night?'*

How looks the night? There does not miss a star.
The million sorts of unaccounted motes
Now quicken, sheathed in the yellow galaxy.
There is no parting or bare interstice
Where the stint compass of a skylark's wings
Would not put out some tiny golden centre.

381 *'Repeat that, repeat'*

Repeat that, repeat,
Cuckoo, bird, and open ear wells, heart-springs, delightfully
    sweet,
With a ballad, with a ballad, a rebound
Off trundled timber and scoops of the hillside ground, hollow
    hollow hollow ground:
The whole landscape flushes on a sudden at a sound.

379 own my] my own   reaving] taking away

156

382   *'Not of all my eyes see'*

Not of all my eyes see, wandering on the world,
Is anything a milk to the mind so, so sighs deep
Poetry tó it, as a tree whose boughs break in the sky.
Say it is áshboughs: whether on a December day and furled
Fast ór they in clammyish lashtender combs creep
Apart wide and new-nestle at heaven most high.

They touch heaven, tabour on it; how their talons sweep
The smouldering enormous winter welkin! May
Mells blue and snowwhite through them, a fringe and fray
Of greenery. it is old earth's groping towards the steep
          Heaven whom she childs us by.

383   *'She schools the flighty pupils of her eyes'*

          She schools the flighty pupils of her eyes,
          With levell'd lashes stilling their disquiet;
          She puts in leash her pair'd lips lest surprise
          Bare the condition of a realm at riot.
          If he suspect that she has ought to sigh at
          His injury she'll avenge with raging shame.
          She kept her love-thoughts on most lenten diet,
          And learnt her not to startle at his name.

384   *The Rainbow*

              See on one hand
          He drops his bright roots in the water'd sward,
          And rosing part, on part dispenses green;
          But with his other foot three miles beyond
          He rises from the flocks of villages
          That bead the plain; did ever Havering church-tower
          Breathe in such ether? or the Quickly elms
          Mask'd with such violet disallow their green?

382 mells] mingles
383 learnt her] taught herself

ROBERT BRIDGES
1844–1930

385   *Triolet*

When first we met we did not guess
That Love would prove so hard a master;
Of more than common friendliness
When first we met we did not guess.
Who could foretell this sore distress,
This irretrievable disaster
When first we met?—We did not guess
That Love would prove so hard a master.

386   *April 1885*

Wanton with long delay the gay spring leaping cometh;
The blackthorn starreth now his bough on the eve of May:
All day in the sweet box-tree the bee for pleasure hummeth:
The cuckoo sends afloat his note on the air all day.

Now dewy nights again and rain in gentle shower
At root of tree and flower have quenched the winter's drouth:
On high the hot sun smiles, and banks of cloud uptower
In bulging heads that crowd for miles the dazzling south.

ALICE MEYNELL
1847–1922

387   *'I Am the Way'*

Thou art the Way.
Hadst Thou been nothing but the goal,
    I cannot say
If Thou hadst ever met my soul.

I cannot see—
I, child of process—if there lies
  An end for me,
Full of repose, full of replies.

  I'll not reproach
The road that winds, my feet that err.
  Access, Approach
Art Thou, Time, Way, and Wayfarer.

388   *The Rainy Summer*

There's much afoot in heaven and earth this year;
  The winds hunt up the sun, hunt up the moon,
Trouble the dubious dawn, hasten the drear
  Height of a threatening noon.

No breath of boughs, no breath of leaves, of fronds,
  May linger or grow warm; the trees are loud;
The forest, rooted, tosses in her bonds,
  And strains against the cloud.

No scents may pause within the garden-fold;
  The rifled flowers are cold as ocean-shells;
Bees, humming in the storm, carry their cold
  Wild honey to cold cells.

389   *Maternity*

One wept whose only child was dead,
New-born, ten years ago.
'Weep not; he is in bliss,' they said.
She answered, 'Even so,

'Ten years ago was born in pain
A child, not now forlorn.
But oh, ten years ago, in vain,
A mother, a mother was born.'

ROBERT LOUIS STEVENSON
1850–1894

390   *'I am a hunchback'*

I am a hunchback, yellow faced,
  A hateful sight to see,
'Tis all that other men can do
  To pass and let me be.

I am a woman, my hair is white,
  I was a darkhaired lass;
The gin dances in my head,
  I stumble as I pass.

I am a man that God made at first,
  And teachers tried to harm,
Here! hunchback take my friendly hand,
  Good woman, take my arm.

FRANCIS COUTTS
1852–1923

391   *On a Wife*

Once I learnt in wilful hour
  How to vex him; still I keep,
Now unwilfully, my power:
  Every day he comes to weep.

FRANCIS WILLIAM BOURDILLON

1852–1921

392   *The Night Has a Thousand Eyes*

The night has a thousand eyes,
    And the day but one;
Yet the light of the bright world dies
    With the dying sun.

The mind has a thousand eyes,
    And the heart but one;
Yet the light of a whole life dies
    When love is gone.

OSCAR WILDE

1854–1900

393   *Symphony in Yellow*

An omnibus across the bridge
    Crawls like a yellow butterfly,
    And, here and there, a passer-by
Shows like a little restless midge.

Big barges full of yellow hay
    Are moored against the shadowy wharf,
    And, like a yellow silken scarf,
The thick fog hangs along the quay.

The yellow leaves begin to fade
    And flutter from the Temple elms,
    And at my feet the pale green Thames
Lies like a rod of rippled jade.

FRANCIS THOMPSON
1859–1907

394   *At Lord's*

It is little I repair to the matches of the Southron folk,
    Though my own red roses there may blow;
It is little I repair to the matches of the Southron folk,
    Though the red roses crest the caps, I know.
For the field is full of shades as I near the shadowy coast,
And a ghostly batsman plays to the bowling of a ghost,
And I look through my tears on a soundless-clapping host
    As the run-stealers flicker to and fro,
      To and fro:—
O my Hornby and my Barlow long ago!

395   *Heaven and Hell*

'Tis said there were no thought of hell,
    Save hell were taught; that there should be
A Heaven for all's self-credible.
    Not so the thing appears to me.
'Tis Heaven that lies beyond our sights,
    And hell too possible that proves;
For all can feel the God that smites,
    But ah, how few the God that loves!

396   *The End of It*

She did not love to love, but hated him
For making her to love; and so her whim
From passion taught misprision to begin.
And all this sin
Was because love to cast out had no skill
Self, which was regent still.
Her own self-will made void her own self's will.

A. E. HOUSMAN
1859–1936

397   *Eight o'Clock*

He stood, and heard the steeple
    Sprinkle the quarters on the morning town.
One, two, three, four, to market-place and people
    It tossed them down.

Strapped, noosed, nighing his hour,
    He stood and counted them and cursed his luck;
And then the clock collected in the tower
    Its strength, and struck.

398   *'The night is freezing fast'*

The night is freezing fast,
    To-morrow comes December;
        And winterfalls of old
Are with me from the past;
    And chiefly I remember
        How Dick would hate the cold.

Fall, winter, fall; for he,
    Prompt hand and headpiece clever,
        Has woven a winter robe,
And made of earth and sea
    His overcoat for ever,
        And wears the turning globe.

399   *'The fairies break their dances'*

The fairies break their dances
    And leave the printed lawn,
And up from India glances
    The silver sail of dawn.

The candles burn their sockets,
　　The blinds let through the day,
The young man feels his pockets
　　And wonders what's to pay.

400　　　　　　　*Revolution*

West and away the wheels of darkness roll,
　　Day's beamy banner up the east is borne,
Spectres and fears, the nightmare and her foal,
　　Drown in the golden deluge of the morn.

But over sea and continent from sight
　　Safe to the Indies has the earth conveyed
The vast and moon-eclipsing cone of night,
　　Her towering foolscap of eternal shade.

See, in mid heaven the sun is mounted; hark,
　　The belfries tingle to the noonday chime.
'Tis silent, and the subterranean dark
　　Has crossed the nadir, and begins to climb.

401　　　　*'Stars, I have seen them fall'*

Stars, I have seen them fall,
　　But when they drop and die
No star is lost at all
　　From all the star-sown sky.
The toil of all that be
　　Helps not the primal fault;
It rains into the sea,
　　And still the sea is salt.

400 foolscap] fool's cap, i.e. conical

402   *'Crossing alone the nighted ferry'*

    Crossing alone the nighted ferry
      With the one coin for fee,
    Whom, on the wharf of Lethe waiting,
      Count you to find? Not me.

    The brisk fond lackey to fetch and carry,
      The true, sick-hearted slave,
    Expect him not in the just city
      And free land of the grave.

403   *'Half-way, for one commandment broken'*

    Half-way, for one commandment broken,
      The woman made her endless halt,
    And she to-day, a glistering token,
      Stands in the wilderness of salt.
    Behind, the vats of judgment brewing
      Thundered, and thick the brimstone snowed;
    He to the hill of his undoing
      Pursued his road.

MARY COLERIDGE

1861–1907

404   *The Nurse's Lament*

    The flower is withered on the stem,
    The fruit hath fallen from the bough.
    None knows nor thinks of them.
    There's no child in the house now.

    The bird that sang sings not here.
    Where is the bonny lark?
    When shall I behold my dear?
    The fire is out, the house dark.

405   *'We never said farewell'*

We never said farewell, nor even looked
   Our last upon each other, for no sign
Was made when we the linkèd chain unhooked
   And broke the level line.

And here we dwell together, side by side,
   Our places fixed for life upon the chart.
Two islands that the roaring seas divide
   Are not more far apart.

406   *'I saw a stable'*

I saw a stable, low and very bare,
   A little child in the manger.
The oxen knew Him, had Him in their care,
   To men He was a stranger.
The safety of the world was lying there,
   And the world's danger.

EDEN PHILLPOTTS
1862–1960

407   *Miniature*

The grey beards wag, the bald heads nod,
And gather thick as bees,
To talk electrons, gases, God,
Old nebulae, new fleas.
Each specialist, each dry-as-dust
And professorial oaf,
Holds up his little crumb of crust
And cries, 'Behold the loaf!'

RUDYARD KIPLING
1865–1936

408   *'Look, you have cast out Love!'*

from *Plain Tales from the Hills ('Lispeth')*

Look, you have cast out Love! What Gods are these
You bid me please?
The Three in One, the One in Three? Not so!
To my own Gods I go.
It may be they shall give me greater ease
Than your cold Christ and tangled Trinities.

409   *'There is a tide'*

from *Plain Tales from the Hills ('Kidnapped')*

There is a tide in the affairs of men
Which, taken any way you please, is bad,
And strands them in forsaken guts and creeks
No decent soul would think of visiting.
You cannot stop the tide; but, now and then,
You may arrest some rash adventurer,
Who—h'm—will hardly thank you for your pains.

410   *A Dead Statesman*

from *Epitaphs of War*

I could not dig: I dared not rob:
Therefore I lied to please the mob.
Now all my lies are proved untrue
And I must face the men I slew.
What tale shall serve me here among
Mine angry and defrauded young?

W. B. YEATS
1865–1939

411   *All Things Can Tempt Me*

All things can tempt me from this craft of verse:
One time it was a woman's face, or worse—
The seeming needs of my fool-driven land;
Now nothing but comes readier to the hand
Than this accustomed toil. When I was young,
I had not given a penny for a song
Did not the poet sing it with such airs
That one believed he had a sword upstairs;
Yet would be now, could I but have my wish,
Colder and dumber and deafer than a fish.

412   *Paudeen*

Indignant at the fumbling wits, the obscure spite
Of our old Paudeen in his shop, I stumbled blind
Among the stones and thorn-trees, under morning light;
Until a curlew cried and in the luminous wind
A curlew answered; and suddenly thereupon I thought
That on the lonely height where all are in God's eye,
There cannot be, confusion of our sound forgot,
A single soul that lacks a sweet crystalline cry.

413 ## *The Cold Heaven*

Suddenly I saw the cold and rook-delighting heaven
That seemed as though ice burned and was but the more ice,
And thereupon imagination and heart were driven
So wild that every casual thought of that and this
Vanished, and left but memories, that should be out of season
With the hot blood of youth, of love crossed long ago;
And I took all the blame out of all sense and reason,
Until I cried and trembled and rocked to and fro,
Riddled with light. Ah! when the ghost begins to quicken,
Confusion of the death-bed over, is it sent
Out naked on the roads, as the books say, and stricken
By the injustice of the skies for punishment?

414 ## *A Coat*

I made my song a coat
Covered with embroideries
Out of old mythologies
From heel to throat;
But the fools caught it,
Wore it in the world's eyes
As though they'd wrought it.
Song, let them take it,
For there's more enterprise
In walking naked.

415 ## *A Thought from Propertius*

She might, so noble from head
To great shapely knees
The long flowing line,
Have walked to the altar
Through the holy images
At Pallas Athene's side,
Or been fit spoil for a centaur
Drunk with the unmixed wine.

169

416 *Death*

Nor dread nor hope attend
A dying animal;
A man awaits his end
Dreading and hoping all;
Many times he died,
Many times rose again.
A great man in his pride
Confronting murderous men
Casts derision upon
Supersession of breath;
He knows death to the bone—
Man has created death.

417 *Spilt Milk*

We that have done and thought,
That have thought and done,
Must ramble, and thin out
Like milk spilt on a stone.

418 *The Choice*

The intellect of man is forced to choose
Perfection of the life, or of the work,
And if it take the second must refuse
A heavenly mansion, raging in the dark.

When all that story's finished, what's the news?
In luck or out the toil has left its mark:
That old perplexity an empty purse,
Or the day's vanity, the night's remorse.

419 *Consolation*

O but there is wisdom
In what the sages said;
But stretch that body for a while
And lay down that head
Till I have told the sages
Where man is comforted.

How could passion run so deep
Had I never thought
That the crime of being born
Blackens all our lot?
But where the crime's committed
The crime can be forgot.

420 *The Great Day*

Hurrah for revolution and more cannon-shot!
A beggar upon horseback lashes a beggar on foot.
Hurrah for revolution and cannon come again!
The beggars have changed places, but the lash goes on.

ARTHUR SYMONS

1865–1945

421 Maquillage

The charm of rouge on fragile cheeks,
Pearl-powder, and, about the eyes,
The dark and lustrous eastern dyes;
A voice of violets that speaks
Of perfumed hours of day, and doubtful night
Of alcoves curtained close against the light.

Gracile and creamy white and rose,
Complexioned like the flower of dawn,
Her fleeting colours are as those
That, from an April sky withdrawn,
Fade in a fragrant mist of tears away
When weeping noon leads on the altered day.

422   *At The Cavour*

Wine, the red coals, the flaring gas,
    Bring out a brighter tone in cheeks
That learn at home before the glass
    The flush that eloquently speaks.

The blue-grey smoke of cigarettes
    Curls from the lessening ends that glow;
The men are thinking of the bets,
    The women of the debts, they owe.

Then their eyes meet, and in their eyes
    The accustomed smile comes up to call,
A look half miserably wise,
    Half heedlessly ironical.

423   *Isolation*

When your lips seek my lips they bring
That sorrowful and outcast thing
My heart home from its wandering.

Then ere your lips have loosed their hold,
I feel my heart's heat growing cold,
And my heart shivers and grows old.

When your lips leave my lips, again
I feel the old doubt and the old pain
Tighten about me like a chain.

After the pain, after the doubt,
A lonely darkness winds about
My soul like death, and shuts you out.

172

424   *Venice*

Water and marble and that silentness
Which is not broken by a wheel or hoof;
A city like a water-lily, less
Seen than reflected, palace wall and roof,
In the unfruitful waters motionless,
Without one living grass's green reproof;
A city without joy or weariness,
Itself beholding, from itself aloof.

ERNEST DOWSON
1867–1900

425   *Epigram*

Because I am idolatrous and have besought,
With grievous supplication and consuming prayer,
The admirable image that my dreams have wrought
Out of her swan's neck and her dark, abundant hair:
The jealous gods, who brook no worship save their own,
Turned my live idol marble and her heart to stone.

426   Vitae Summa Brevis Spem Nos Vetat
Incohare Longam

They are not long, the weeping and the laughter,
    Love and desire and hate:
I think they have no portion in us after
    We pass the gate.

They are not long, the days of wine and roses:
    Out of a misty dream
Our path emerges for a while, then closes
    Within a dream.

426 title] Life's short span forbids us to enter on far-reaching hopes. (Horace)

GEORGE RUSSELL (AE)
1867–1935

427   *Outcast*

Sometimes when alone
At the dark close of day,
Men meet an outlawed majesty
And hurry away.

They come to the lighted house;
They talk to their dear;
They crucify the mystery
With words of good cheer.

When love and life are over,
And flight's at an end,
On the outcast majesty
They lean as a friend.

CHARLOTTE MEW
1869–1928

428   *Beside the Bed*

Someone has shut the shining eyes, straightened and folded
    The wandering hands quietly covering the unquiet breast:
So, smoothed and silenced you lie, like a child not again to be
        questioned or scolded;
    But, for you, not one of us believes that this is rest.

Not so to close the windows down can cloud and deaden
    The blue beyond: or to screen the wavering flame subdue its
        breath:
Why, if I lay my cheek to your cheek, your grey lips, like dawn,
        would quiver and redden,
    Breaking into the old, odd smile at this fraud of death.

174

Because all night you have not turned to us or spoken
   It is time for you to wake; your dreams were never very deep:
I, for one, have seen the thin, bright, twisted threads of them
     dimmed suddenly and broken,
   This is only a most piteous pretence of sleep!

EDWIN ARLINGTON ROBINSON
1869–1935

429   *An Old Story*

     Strange that I did not know him then,
       That friend of mine!
     I did not even show him then
       One friendly sign;

     But cursed him for the ways he had
       To make me see
     My envy of the praise he had
       For praising me.

     I would have rid the earth of him
       Once, in my pride . . .
     I never knew the worth of him
       Until he died.

430   *Exit*

For what we owe to other days,
Before we poisoned him with praise,
May we who shrank to find him weak
Remember that he cannot speak.

For envy that we may recall,
And for our faith before the fall,
May we who are alive be slow
To tell what we shall never know.

For penance he would not confess,
And for the fateful emptiness
Of early triumph undermined,
May we now venture to be kind.

HILAIRE BELLOC
1870–1953

431   *The Early Morning*

The moon on the one hand, the dawn on the other:
The moon is my sister, the dawn is my brother.
The moon on my left hand and the dawn on my right.
My brother, good morning: my sister, good night.

432   *Discovery*

Life is a long discovery, isn't it?
You only get your wisdom bit by bit.
If you have luck you find in early youth
How dangerous it is to tell the Truth;
And next you learn how dignity and peace
Are the ripe fruits of patient avarice.
You find that middle life goes racing past.
You find despair: and, at the very last,
You find as you are giving up the ghost
That those who loved you best despised you most.

433   *The False Heart*

I said to Heart, 'How goes it?' Heart replied:
'Right as a Ribstone Pippin!' But it lied.

STEPHEN CRANE
1871–1900

434   *'In the desert'*

In the desert
I saw a creature, naked, bestial,
Who, squatting upon the ground,
Held his heart in his hands,
And ate of it.
I said, 'Is it good, friend?'
'It is bitter—bitter,' he answered;
'But I like it
Because it is bitter,
And because it is my heart.'

435   *'A god in wrath'*

A god in wrath
Was beating a man;
He cuffed him loudly
With thunderous blows
That rang and rolled over the earth.
All people came running.
The man screamed and struggled,
And bit madly at the feet of the god.
The people cried:
'Ah, what a wicked man!'
And—
'Ah, what a redoubtable god!'

436   *'A man said'*

A man said to the universe:
'Sir, I exist!'
'However,' replied the universe,
'The fact has not created in me
A sense of obligation.'

J. M. SYNGE
1871–1909

437   *On an Island*

You've pluck'd a curlew, drawn a hen,
Wash'd the shirts of seven men,
You've stuff'd my pillow, stretch'd the sheet,
And fill'd the pan to wash your feet,
You've coop'd the pullets, wound the clock,
And rinsed the young men's drinking crock;
And now we'll dance to jigs and reels,
Nailed boots chasing girls' naked heels,
Until your father'll start to snore,
And Jude, now you're married, will stretch on the floor.

438   *Dread*

Beside a chapel I'd a room looked down,
Where all the women from the farms and town,
On Holy-days and Sundays used to pass
To marriages, and christenings, and to Mass.

Then I sat lonely watching score and score,
Till I turned jealous of the Lord next door. . . .
Now by this window, where there's none can see,
The Lord God's jealous of yourself and me.

W. H. DAVIES
1871–1940

439   *I Am the Poet Davies, William*

I am the Poet Davies, William,
  I sin without a blush or blink:
I am a man that lives to eat;
  I am a man that lives to drink.

178

My face is large, my lips are thick,
  My skin is coarse and black almost;
But the ugliest feature is my verse,
  Which proves my soul is black and lost.

Thank heaven thou didst not marry me,
  A poet full of blackest evil;
For how to manage my damned soul
  Will puzzle many a flaming devil.

440
The Villain

While joy gave clouds the light of stars,
  That beamed where'er they looked;
And calves and lambs had tottering knees,
  Excited, while they sucked;
While every bird enjoyed his song,
Without one thought of harm or wrong—
I turned my head and saw the wind,
  Not far from where I stood,
Dragging the corn by her golden hair,
  Into a dark and lonely wood.

441
D is for Dog

My dog went mad and bit my hand,
  I was bitten to the bone:
My wife went walking out with him,
  And then came back alone.

I smoked my pipe, I nursed my wound,
  I saw them both depart:
And when my wife came back alone,
  I was bitten to the heart.

W. H. DAVIES

442   *All in June*

A week ago I had a fire,
  To warm my feet, my hands and face;
Cold winds, that never make a friend,
  Crept in and out of every place.

Today, the fields are rich in grass,
  And buttercups in thousands grow;
I'll show the World where I have been—
  With gold-dust seen on either shoe.

Till to my garden back I come,
  Where bumble-bees, for hours and hours,
Sit on their soft, fat, velvet bums,
  To wriggle out of hollow flowers.

RALPH HODGSON

1871–1962

443   *The Bells of Heaven*

'Twould ring the bells of Heaven
The wildest peal for years,
If Parson lost his senses
And people came to theirs,
And he and they together
Knelt down with angry prayers
For tamed and shabby tigers
And dancing dogs and bears,
And wretched, blind pit ponies,
And little hunted hares.

444   *'Reason has moons'*

Reason has moons, but moons not hers
  Lie mirror'd on her sea,
Confounding her astronomers,
  But, O! delighting me.

180

FORD MADOX FORD

1873–1939

445   Sidera Cadentia

On the Death of Queen Victoria

When one of the old, little stars doth fall from its place,
    The eye,
Glimpsing aloft must sadden to see that its space
    In the sky
Is darker, lacking a spot of its ancient, shimmering grace,
And sadder, a little, for loss of the glimmer on high.

Very remote, a glitter, a mote far away, is your star,
But its glint being gone from the place where it shone
The night's somewhat grimmer and something is gone
Out of the comforting quiet of things as they are.

    A shock,
A change in the beat of the clock;
And the ultimate change that we fear feels a little less far.

WALTER DE LA MARE

1873–1956

446   *Arrogance*

I saw bleak Arrogance, with brows of brass,
Clad nape to sole in shimmering foil of lead,
Stark down his nose he stared; a crown of glass
Aping the rainbow, on his tilted head.

445 title] Falling Stars

His very presence drained the vital air;
He sate erect—stone-cold, self-crucified;
On either side of him an empty chair;
And sawdust trickled from his wounded side.

447   *The Spotted Flycatcher*

Gray on gray post, this silent little bird
Swoops on its prey—prey neither seen nor heard!
A click of bill; a flicker; and, back again!
Sighs Nature an *Alas*? Or merely, *Amen*?

448   *The Owl*

Apart, thank Heaven, from all to do
To keep alive the long day through;
To imagine; think; watch; listen to;
There still remains—the heart to bless,
Exquisite pregnant Idleness.

Why, we might let all else go by
To seek its Essence till we die . . .

Hark, now! that Owl, a-snoring in his tree,
Till it grow dark enough for him to see.

449   *Crazed*

I know a pool where nightshade preens
Her poisonous fruitage in the moon;
Where the frail aspen her shadow leans
In midnight cold a-swoon.

I know a meadow flat with gold—
A million million burning flowers
In noon-sun's thirst their buds unfold
Beneath his blazing showers.

I saw a crazèd face, did I,
Stare from the lattice of a mill,
While the lank sails clacked idly by
High on the windy hill.

TRUMBULL STICKNEY
1874–1904

450   *'Sir, say no more'*

Sir, say no more.
Within me 't is as if
The green and climbing eyesight of a cat
Crawled near my mind's poor birds.

G. K. CHESTERTON
1874–1936

451   *Elegy in a Country Churchyard*

The men that worked for England
They have their graves at home:
And bees and birds of England
About the cross can roam.

But they that fought for England,
Following a falling star,
Alas, alas for England
They have their graves afar.

And they that rule in England,
In stately conclave met,
Alas, alas for England
They have no graves as yet.

452 *Ecclesiastes*

There is one sin: to call a green leaf grey,
    Whereat the sun in heaven shuddereth.
There is one blasphemy: for death to pray,
    For God alone knoweth the praise of death.

There is one creed: 'neath no world-terror's wing
    Apples forget to grow on apple-trees.
There is one thing is needful—everything—
    The rest is vanity of vanities.

ROBERT FROST

1874–1963

453 *In Neglect*

They leave us so to the way we took,
    As two in whom they were proved mistaken,
That we sit sometimes in the wayside nook,
With mischievous, vagrant, seraphic look,
And *try* if we cannot feel forsaken.

454 *A Patch of Old Snow*

There's a patch of old snow in a corner
    That I should have guessed
Was a blow-away paper the rain
    Had brought to rest.

It is speckled with grime as if
    Small print overspread it,
The news of a day I've forgotten—
    If I ever read it.

455 *The Cow in Apple-Time*

Something inspires the only cow of late
To make no more of a wall than an open gate,
And think no more of wall-builders than fools.
Her face is flecked with pomace and she drools
A cider syrup. Having tasted fruit,
She scorns a pasture withering to the root.
She runs from tree to tree where lie and sweeten
The windfalls spiked with stubble and worm-eaten.
She leaves them bitten when she has to fly.
She bellows on a knoll against the sky.
Her udder shrivels and the milk goes dry.

456 *The Line-Gang*

Here come the line-gang pioneering by.
They throw a forest down less cut than broken.
They plant dead trees for living, and the dead
They string together with a living thread.
They string an instrument against the sky
Wherein words whether beaten out or spoken
Will run as hushed as when they were a thought
But in no hush they string it: they go past
With shouts afar to pull the cable taut,
To hold it hard until they make it fast,
To ease away—they have it. With a laugh,
An oath of towns that set the wild at naught
They bring the telephone and telegraph.

457 *Dust of Snow*

The way a crow
Shook down on me
The dust of snow
From a hemlock tree

Has given my heart
A change of mood
And saved some part
Of a day I had rued.

185

458 *Fireflies in the Garden*

Here come real stars to fill the upper skies,
And here on earth come emulating flies,
That though they never equal stars in size,
(And they were never really stars at heart)
Achieve at times a very star-like start.
Only, of course, they can't sustain the part.

459 *The Armful*

For every parcel I stoop down to seize,
I lose some other off my arms and knees,
And the whole pile is slipping, bottles, buns,
Extremes too hard to comprehend at once,
Yet nothing I should care to leave behind.
With all I have to hold with, hand and mind
And heart, if need be, I will do my best
To keep their building balanced at my breast.
I crouch down to prevent them as they fall;
Then sit down in the middle of them all.
I had to drop the armful in the road
And try to stack them in a better load.

460 *Were I in Trouble*

Where I could think of no thoroughfare,
Away on the mountain up far too high,
A blinding headlight shifted glare
And began to bounce down a granite stair
Like a star fresh fallen out of the sky.
And I away in my opposite wood
Am touched by that unintimate light
And made feel less alone than I rightly should,
For traveller there could do me no good
Were I in trouble with night tonight.

ROBERT FROST

461   *A Mood Apart*

Once down on my knees to growing plants
I prodded the earth with a lazy tool
In time with a medley of sotto chants;
But becoming aware of some boys from school
Who had stopped outside the fence to spy,
I stopped my song and almost heart,
For any eye is an evil eye
That looks in on to a mood apart.

EDWARD THOMAS

1878–1917

462   *'She had a name'*

She had a name among the children;
But no one loved though someone owned
Her, locked her out of doors at bedtime
And had her kittens duly drowned.

In Spring, nevertheless, this cat
Ate blackbirds, thrushes, nightingales,
And birds of bright voice and plume and flight,
As well as scraps from neighbours' pails.

I loathed and hated her for this;
One speckle on a thrush's breast
Was worth a million such; and yet
She lived long, till God gave her rest.

463 *Cock-Crow*

Out of the wood of thoughts that grows by night
To be cut down by the sharp axe of light,—
Out of the night, two cocks together crow,
Cleaving the darkness with a silver blow:
And bright before my eyes twin trumpeters stand,
Heralds of splendour, one at either hand,
Each facing each as in a coat of arms:
The milkers lace their boots up at the farms.

464 *Thaw*

Over the land freckled with snow half-thawed
The speculating rooks at their nests cawed
And saw from elm-tops, delicate as flower of grass,
What we below could not see, Winter pass.

465 *Tall Nettles*

Tall nettles cover up, as they have done
These many springs, the rusty harrow, the plough
Long worn out, and the roller made of stone:
Only the elm butt tops the nettles now.

This corner of the farmyard I like most:
As well as any bloom upon a flower
I like the dust on the nettles, never lost
Except to prove the sweetness of a shower.

466 *'By the ford'*

By the ford at the town's edge
Horse and carter rest:
The carter smokes on the bridge
Watching the water press in swathes about his
    horse's chest.

From the inn one watches, too,
In the room for visitors
That has no fire, but a view
And many cases of stuffed fish, vermin, and
      kingfishers.

CARL SANDBURG
1878–1967

467   *Cool Tombs*

When Abraham Lincoln was shoveled into the tombs, he forgot
    the copperheads and the assassin . . . in the dust, in the cool
    tombs.

And Ulysses Grant lost all thought of con men and Wall Street,
    cash and collateral turned ashes . . . in the dust, in the cool
    tombs.

Pocahontas' body, lovely as a poplar, sweet as a red haw in
    November or a pawpaw in May, did she wonder? does she
    remember? . . . in the dust, in the cool tombs?

Take any streetful of people buying clothes and groceries, cheering
    a hero or throwing confetti and blowing tin horns . . . tell me if
    the lovers are losers . . . tell me if any get more than the lovers
    . . . in the dust . . . in the cool tombs.

VACHEL LINDSAY
1879–1931

468   *The Leaden-Eyed*

Let not young souls be smothered out before
They do quaint deeds and fully flaunt their pride.
It is the world's one crime its babes grow dull,
Its poor are ox-like, limp and leaden-eyed.

Not that they starve, but starve so dreamlessly,
Not that they sow, but that they seldom reap,
Not that they serve, but have no gods to serve,
Not that they die, but that they die like sheep.

469   *What the Moon Saw*

Two statesmen met by moonlight.
Their ease was partly feigned.
They glanced about the prairie.
Their faces were constrained.
In various ways aforetime
They had misled the state,
Yet did it so politely
Their henchmen thought them great.
They sat beneath a hedge and spake
No word, but had a smoke.
A satchel passed from hand to hand.
Next day, the deadlock broke.

470   *Factory Windows Are Always Broken*

Factory windows are always broken.
Somebody's always throwing bricks,
Somebody's always heaving cinders,
Playing ugly Yahoo tricks.

VACHEL LINDSAY

Factory windows are always broken.
Other windows are let alone.
No one throws through the chapel-window
The bitter, snarling derisive stone.

Factory windows are always broken.
Something or other is going wrong.
Something is rotten—I think, in Denmark.
End of the factory-window song.

WALLACE STEVENS
1879–1955

471   *Anecdote of the Jar*

I placed a jar in Tennessee,
And round it was, upon a hill.
It made the slovenly wilderness
Surround that hill.

The wilderness rose up to it,
And sprawled around, no longer wild.
The jar was round upon the ground
And tall and of a port in air.

It took dominion everywhere.
The jar was gray and bare.
It did not give of bird or bush,
Like nothing else in Tennessee.

472   *The Death of a Soldier*

Life contracts and death is expected,
As in a season of autumn.
The soldier falls.

He does not become a three-days personage,
Imposing his separation,
Calling for pomp.

Death is absolute and without memorial,
As in a season of autumn,
When the wind stops,

When the wind stops and, over the heavens,
The clouds go, nevertheless,
In their direction.

473   *Men Made Out of Words*

What should we be without the sexual myth,
The human revery or poem of death?

Castratos of moon-mash—Life consists
Of propositions about life. The human

Revery is a solitude in which
We compose these propositions, torn by dreams,

By the terrible incantations of defeats
And by the fear that defeats and dreams are one.

The whole race is a poet that writes down
The eccentric propositions of its fate.

JOHN FREEMAN
1880–1929

474   *The Hounds*

Far off a lonely hound
Telling his loneliness all round
To the dark woods, dark hills, and darker sea;

And, answering, the sound
Of that yet lonelier sea-hound
Telling his loneliness to the solitary stars.

Hearing, the kennelled hound
Some neighbourhood and comfort found,
And slept beneath the comfortless high stars.

But that wild sea-hound
Unkennelled, called all night all round—
The unneighboured and uncomforted cold sea.

JAMES STEPHENS
1882–1950

475   *A Glass of Beer*

The lanky hank of a she in the inn over there
Nearly killed me for asking the loan of a glass of beer;
May the devil grip the whey-faced slut by the hair,
And beat bad manners out of her skin for a year.

That parboiled ape, with the toughest jaw you will see
On virtue's path, and a voice that would rasp the dead,
Came roaring and raging the minute she looked at me,
And threw me out of the house on the back of my head!

If I asked her master he'd give me a cask a day;
But she, with the beer at hand, not a gill would arrange!
May she marry a ghost and bear him a kitten, and may
The High King of Glory permit her to get the mange.

T. E. HULME
1883–1917

476

The Embankment

*(The Fantasia of a Fallen Gentleman
on a Cold, Bitter Night)*

Once, in finesse of fiddles found I ecstasy,
In a flash of gold heels on the hard pavement.
Now see I
That warmth's the very stuff of poesy.
Oh, God, make small
The old star-eaten blanket of the sky,
That I may fold it round me and in comfort lie.

477

Conversion

Light-hearted I walked into the valley wood
In the time of hyacinths,
Till beauty like a scented cloth
Cast over, stifled me, I was bound
Motionless and faint of breath
By loveliness that is her own eunuch.
Now pass I to the final river
Ignominiously, in a sack, without sound,
As any peeping Turk to the Bosphorus.

WILLIAM CARLOS WILLIAMS
1883–1963

478
A Sort of a Song

Let the snake wait under
his weed
and the writing
be of words, slow and quick, sharp
to strike, quiet to wait,
sleepless.

—through metaphor to reconcile
the people and the stones.
Compose. (No ideas
but in things) Invent!
Saxifrage is my flower that splits
the rocks.

479
The Hard Listener

The powerless emperor
makes himself dull
writing poems in a garden
while his armies
kill and burn. But we,
in poverty lacking love,
keep some relation
to the truth of man's
infelicity: say
the late flowers, unspoiled
by insects and waiting
only for the cold.

JAMES ELROY FLECKER

1884–1915

480   *No Coward's Song*

I am afraid to think about my death,
When it shall be, and whether in great pain
I shall rise up and fight the air for breath
Or calmly wait the bursting of my brain.

I am no coward who could seek in fear
A folk-lore solace or sweet Indian tales:
I know dead men are deaf and cannot hear
The singing of a thousand nightingales.

I know dead men are blind and cannot see
The friend that shuts in horror their big eyes,
And they are witless—O, I'd rather be
A living mouse than dead as a man dies.

ANNA WICKHAM

1884–1947

481   *Gift to a Jade*

For love he offered me his perfect world.
This world was so constricted and so small
It had no sort of loveliness at all,
And I flung back the little silly ball.
At that cold moralist I hotly hurled
His perfect, pure, symmetrical, small world.

482 *Soul's Liberty*

He who has lost soul's liberty
Concerns himself for ever with his property,
As, when the folk have lost both dance and song,
Women clean useless pots the whole day long.

Thank God for war and fire
To burn the silly objects of desire,
That, from the ruin of a church thrown down,
We see God clear and high above the town.

SIR JOHN SQUIRE
1884–1958

483 *Interior*

I and myself swore enmity. Alack,
Myself has tied my hands behind my back.
Yielding, I know there's no excuse in them—
I was accomplice to the stratagem.

ELINOR WYLIE
1885–1928

484 *Let No Charitable Hope*

Now let no charitable hope
Confuse my mind with images
Of eagle and of antelope:
I am in nature none of these.

I was, being human, born alone;
I am, being woman, hard beset;
I live by squeezing from a stone
The little nourishment I get.

In masks outrageous and austere
The years go by in single file;
But none has merited my fear,
And none has quite escaped my smile.

485   *Cold-Blooded Creatures*

Man, the egregious egoist
(In mystery the twig is bent),
Imagines, by some mental twist,
That he alone is sentient

Of the intolerable load
Which on all living creatures lies,
Nor stoops to pity in the toad
The speechless sorrow of its eyes.

He asks no questions of the snake,
Nor plumbs the phosphorescent gloom
Where lidless fishes, broad awake,
Swim staring at a night-mare doom.

D. H. LAWRENCE
1885–1930

486   *Piano*

Softly, in the dusk, a woman is singing to me;
Taking me back down the vista of years, till I see
A child sitting under the piano, in the boom of the tingling
    strings
And pressing the small, poised feet of a mother who smiles as
    she sings.

In spite of myself, the insidious mastery of song
Betrays me back, till the heart of me weeps to belong
To the old Sunday evenings at home, with winter outside
And hymns in the cosy parlour, the tinkling piano our guide.

So now it is vain for the singer to burst into clamour
With the great black piano appassionato. The glamour
Of childish days is upon me, my manhood is cast
Down in the flood of remembrance, I weep like a child for the
    past.

487   *I Am Like a Rose*

I am myself at last; now I achieve
My very self. I, with the wonder mellow,
Full of fine warmth, I issue forth in clear
And single me, perfected from my fellow.

Here I am all myself. No rose-bush heaving
Its limpid sap to culmination has brought
Itself more sheer and naked out of the green
In stark-clear roses, than I to myself am brought.

488   *Glory*

Glory is of the sun, too, and the sun of suns,
and down the shafts of his splendid pinions
run tiny rivers of peace.

Most of his time, the tiger pads and slouches in a burning
    peace.
And the small hawk high up turns round on the slow pivot of
    peace.
Peace comes from behind the sun, with the peregrine falcon,
    and the owl.
Yet all of these drink blood.

489   *What Would You Fight For?*

I am not sure I would always fight for my life.
Life might not be worth fighting for.

I am not sure I would always fight for my wife.
A wife isn't always worth fighting for.

Nor my children, nor my country, nor my fellow-men.
It all depends whether I found them worth fighting for.

The only thing men invariably fight for
is their money. But I doubt if I'd fight for mine, anyhow
    not to shed a lot of blood over it.

Yet one thing I do fight for, tooth and nail, all the time.
And that is my bit of inward peace, where I am at one
    with myself.

And I must say, I am often worsted.

490   *To Women, As Far As I'm*
                  Concerned

The feelings I don't have I don't have.
The feelings I don't have, I won't say I have.
The feelings you say you have, you don't have.
The feelings you would like us both to have, we
    neither of us have.
The feelings people ought to have, they never have.
If people say they've got feelings, you may be pretty
    sure they haven't got them.
So if you want either of us to feel anything at all
you'd better abandon all idea of feelings altogether.

491   *Intimates*

Don't you care for my love? she said bitterly.

I handed her the mirror, and said:
Please address these questions to the proper person!
Please make all requests to head-quarters!
In all matters of emotional importance
please approach the supreme authority direct!—
So I handed her the mirror.

And she would have broken it over my head,
but she caught sight of her own reflection
and that held her spellbound for two seconds
while I fled.

ANDREW YOUNG

1885–1971

492   *In Teesdale*

No, not tonight,
Not by this fading light,
Not by those high fells where the forces
Fall from the mist like the white tails of horses.

From that dark slack
Where peat-hags gape too black
I turn to where the lighted farm
Holds out through the open door a golden arm.

No, not tonight,
Tomorrow by daylight;
Tonight I fear the fabulous horses
Whose white tails flash down the steep watercourses.

493   *A Dead Mole*

Strong-shouldered mole,
That so much lived below the ground,
Dug, fought and loved, hunted and fed,
For you to raise a mound
Was as for us to make a hole;
What wonder now that being dead
Your body lies here, stout and square
Buried within the blue vault of the air?

492 forces] waterfalls

201

494   *Ba Cottage*

There at the watershed I turned
And looked back at the house I burned—
Burnt, too, by many another tramp
Who sought its shelter, dry or damp.

For coming from the mist-thick moor
I made the window-sill my door
And, wet incendiary, tore up wood
And fed the grate's wide mouth with food.

Then leaning on the mantelshelf
As though a mountain now myself
I smoked with mist and dripped with rain
That slowly made me dry again.

EZRA POUND

1885–1972

495   *The Garden*

En robe de parade. Samain

Like a skein of loose silk blown against a wall
She walks by the railing of a path in Kensington Gardens,
And she is dying piece-meal
          of a sort of emotional anaemia.

And round about there is a rabble
Of the filthy, sturdy, unkillable infants of the very poor.
They shall inherit the earth.

In her is the end of breeding.
Her boredom is exquisite and excessive.
She would like some one to speak to her,
And is almost afraid that I
          will commit that indiscretion.

496 *The Lake Isle*

O God, O Venus, O Mercury, patron of thieves,
Give me in due time, I beseech you, a little tobacco-shop,
With the little bright boxes
    piled up neatly upon the shelves
And the loose fragrant cavendish
    and the shag,
And the bright Virginia
    loose under the bright glass cases,
And a pair of scales not too greasy,
And the whores dropping in for a word or two in passing,
For a flip word, and to tidy their hair a bit.

O God, O Venus, O Mercury, patron of thieves,
Lend me a little tobacco-shop,
    or install me in any profession
Save this damn'd profession of writing,
    where one needs one's brains all the time.

FRANCES CORNFORD
1886–1960

497 *Childhood*

I used to think that grown-up people chose
To have stiff backs and wrinkles round their nose,
And veins like small fat snakes on either hand,
On purpose to be grand.
Till through the banisters I watched one day
My great-aunt Etty's friend who was going away,
And how her onyx beads had come unstrung.
I saw her grope to find them as they rolled;
And then I knew that she was helplessly old,
As I was helplessly young.

498

All Souls' Night

My love came back to me
Under the November tree
Shelterless and dim.
He put his hand upon my shoulder,
He did not think me strange or older,
Nor I, him.

SIEGFRIED SASSOON
1886–1967

499

'Blighters'

The House is crammed: tier beyond tier they grin
And cackle at the Show, while prancing ranks
Of harlots shrill the chorus, drunk with din;
'We're sure the Kaiser loves our dear old Tanks!'

I'd like to see a Tank come down the stalls,
Lurching to rag-time tunes, or 'Home, sweet Home',
And there'd be no more jokes in Music-halls
To mock the riddled corpses round Bapaume.

500

Base Details

If I were fierce, and bald, and short of breath,
  I'd live with scarlet Majors at the Base,
And speed glum heroes up the line to death.
  You'd see me with my puffy petulant face,
Guzzling and gulping in the best hotel,
  Reading the Roll of Honour. 'Poor young chap,'
I'd say—'I used to know his father well;
  Yes, we've lost heavily in this last scrap.'
And when the war is done and youth stone dead,
I'd toddle safely home and die—in bed.

SIEGFRIED SASSOON

501 *The General*

'Good-morning; good-morning!' the General said
When we met him last week on our way to the line.
Now the soldiers he smiled at are most of 'em dead,
And we're cursing his staff for incompetent swine.
'He's a cheery old card,' grunted Harry to Jack
As they slogged up to Arras with rifle and pack.

But he did for them both by his plan of attack.

502 *Everyone Sang*

Everyone suddenly burst out singing;
And I was filled with such delight
As prisoned birds must find in freedom,
Winging wildly across the white
Orchards and dark-green fields; on—on—and out of
    sight.

Everyone's voice was suddenly lifted;
And beauty came like the setting sun:
My heart was shaken with tears; and horror
Drifted away ... O, but Everyone
Was a bird; and the song was wordless; the singing will
    never be done.

503 *'In me, past, present, future meet'*

In me, past, present, future meet
To hold long chiding conference.
My lusts usurp the present tense
And strangle Reason in his seat.
My loves leap through the future's fence
To dance with dream-enfranchised feet.

In me the cave-man clasps the seer,
And garlanded Apollo goes
Chanting to Abraham's deaf ear.
In me the tiger sniffs the rose.
    Look in my heart, kind friends, and tremble,
    Since there your elements assemble.

205

ROBINSON JEFFERS
1887–1962

504   Ave Caesar

No bitterness: our ancestors did it.
They were only ignorant and hopeful, they wanted freedom but
   wealth too.
Their children will learn to hope for a Caesar.
Or rather—for we are not aquiline Romans but soft mixed
   colonists—
Some kindly Sicilian tyrant who'll keep
Poverty and Carthage off until the Romans arrive.
We are easy to manage, a gregarious people,
Full of sentiment, clever at mechanics, and we love our luxuries.

505   *Eagle Valor, Chicken Mind*

Unhappy country, what wings you have! Even here,
Nothing important to protect, and ocean-far from the nearest
     enemy, what a cloud
Of bombers amazes the coast mountain, what a hornet-swarm
     of fighters,
And day and night the guns practicing

Unhappy, eagle wings and beak, chicken brain.
Weep (it is frequent in human affairs), weep for that terrible
     magnificence of the means,
The ridiculous incompetence of the reasons, the bloody and
     shabby
Pathos of the result.

504 title] Hail Caesar!

EDITH SITWELL
1887–1964

506   *Bells of Grey Crystal*

Bells of grey crystal
Break on each bough—
The swans' breath will mist all
The cold airs now.
Like tall pagodas
Two people go,
Trail their long codas
Of talk through the snow.
Lonely are these
And lonely am I. . . .
The clouds, grey Chinese geese,
Sleek through the sky.

MARIANNE MOORE
1887–1972

507   *Poetry*

I, too, dislike it.
     Reading it, however, with a perfect contempt for it, one
       discovers in
it, after all, a place for the genuine.

508   *A Face*

'I am not treacherous, callous, jealous, superstitious,
supercilious, venomous, or absolutely hideous':
     studying and studying its expression,
     exasperated desperation
       though at no real impasse,
       would gladly break the glass;

MARIANNE MOORE

when love of order, ardour, uncircuitous simplicity,
with an expression of inquiry, are all one needs to be!
  Certain faces, a few, one or two—or one
  face photographed by recollection—
    to my mind, to my sight,
    must remain a delight.

509   *I May, I Might, I Must*

        If you will tell me why the fen
        appears impassable, I then
        will tell you why I think that I
        can get across it if I try.

510   *A Jellyfish*

        Visible, invisible,
          a fluctuating charm
        an amber-tinctured amethyst
          inhabits it, your arm
        approaches and it opens
          and it closes; you had meant
        to catch it and it quivers;
          you abandon your intent.

            T. S. ELIOT
            1888–1965

511   *Cousin Nancy*

        Miss Nancy Ellicott
        Strode across the hills and broke them,
        Rode across the hills and broke them—
        The barren New England hills—
        Riding to hounds
        Over the cow-pasture.

208

Miss Nancy Ellicott smoked
And danced all the modern dances;
And her aunts were not quite sure how they felt about it,
But they knew that it was modern.

Upon the glazen shelves kept watch
Matthew and Waldo, guardians of the faith,
The army of unalterable law.

JOHN CROWE RANSOM
1888–1974

512   *Emily Hardcastle, Spinster*

We shall come tomorrow morning, who were not to have her
   love,
We shall bring no face of envy but a gift of praise and lilies
To the stately ceremonial we are not the heroes of.

Let the sisters now attend her, who are red-eyed, who are
   wroth;
They were younger, she was finer, for they wearied of the
   waiting
And they married them to merchants, being unbelievers both.

I was dapper when I dangled in my pepper-and-salt;
We were only local beauties, and we beautifully trusted
If the proud one had to tarry, one would have her by default.

But right across the threshold has her grizzled Baron come;
Let them robe her, Bride and Princess, who'll go down a leafy
   archway
And seal her to the Stranger for his castle in the gloom.

IVOR GURNEY

1890–1937

513   *After War*

One got peace of heart at last, the dark march over,
And the straps slipped, the warmth felt under roof's low cover,
Lying slack the body, let sink in straw giving;
And some sweetness, a great sweetness felt in mere living.
And to come to this haven after sorefooted weeks,
The dark barn roof, and the glows and the wedges and streaks;
Letters from home, dry warmth and still sure rest taken
Sweet to the chilled frame, nerves soothed were so sore shaken.

514   *On the Night*

On the night there are shown dim few stars timorous
And light is smothered in a cloak of fear.
Are these hills out? Then night has brooded there
Of dark things till they were no more for us.

Gone are the strict falls, there is no skyline boundary,
The stars are not resting or coming to rest.
What will dawn show? A land breathing calm of breast,
Or a frightened rook-wheeling plain once bed of the sea?

515   *The Escape*

I believe in the increasing of life: whatever
Leads to the seeing of small trifles,
Real, beautiful, is good; and an act never
Is worthier than in freeing spirit that stifles
Under ingratitude's weight, nor is anything done
Wiselier than the moving or breaking to sight
Of a thing hidden under by custom—revealed,
Fulfilled, used (sound-fashioned) any way out to delight:
Trefoil—hedge sparrow—the stars on the edge at night.

516   *Moments*

I think the loathed minutes one by one
That tear and then go past are little worth
Save nearer to the blindness to the sun
They bring me, and the farewell to all earth

Save to that six-foot length I must lie in
Sodden with mud, and not to grieve again
Because high autumn goes beyond my pen
And snow lies inexprest in the deep lane.

EDNA ST VINCENT MILLAY
1892–1950

517   *Never May the Fruit Be Plucked*

Never, never may the fruit be plucked from the bough
And gathered into barrels.
He that would eat of love must eat it where it hangs.
Though the branches bend like reeds,
Though the ripe fruit splash in the grass or wrinkle on the
    tree,
He that would eat of love may bear away with him
Only what his belly can hold,
Nothing in the apron,
Nothing in the pockets.
Never, never may the fruit be gathered from the bough
And harvested in barrels.
The winter of love is a cellar of empty bins,
In an orchard soft with rot.

518   *To a Young Poet*

Time cannot break the bird's wing from the bird.
Bird and wing together
Go down, one feather.

No thing that ever flew,
Not the lark, not you,
Can die as others do.

519   *The True Encounter*

'Wolf!' cried my cunning heart
At every sheep it spied,
And roused the countryside.

'Wolf! Wolf!'—and up would start
Good neighbours, bringing spade
And pitchfork to my aid.

At length my cry was known:
    Therein lay my release.
I met the wolf alone
    And was devoured in peace.

HUGH MacDIARMID
1892–1978

520   *One of the Principal Causes of War*

O she was full of loving fuss
When I cut my hand and the blood gushed out
And cleverly she dressed the wound
And wrapt it in a clout.

HUGH MACDIARMID

O tenderly she tended me
Though deep in her eyes I could tell
The secret joy that men are whiles
Obliged to bleed as well.

I thanked her kindly and never let on,
Seeing she could not understand,
That she wished me a wound far worse to staunch—
And not in the hand!

WILFRED OWEN
1893–1918

521 *Arms and the Boy*

Let the boy try along this bayonet-blade
How cold steel is, and keen with hunger of blood;
Blue with all malice, like a madman's flash;
And thinly drawn with famishing for flesh.

Lend him to stroke these blind, blunt bullet-leads
Which long to nuzzle in the hearts of lads,
Or give him cartridges whose fine zinc teeth
Are sharp with sharpness of grief and death.

For his teeth seem for laughing round an apple.
There lurk no claws behind his fingers supple;
And God will grow no talons at his heels,
Nor antlers through the thickness of his curls.

RICHARD CHURCH
1893–1972

522   *Be Frugal*

Be frugal in the gift of love,
Lest you should kindle in return
Love like your own, that may survive
Long after yours has ceased to burn.

For in life's later years you may
Meet with the ghost of what you woke
And shattered at a second stroke.
God help you on that fatal day.

E. E. CUMMINGS
1894–1962

523   *'Buffalo Bill's'*

Buffalo Bill's
defunct
            who used to
            ride a watersmooth-silver
                                    stallion
and break onetwothreefourfive pigeonsjustlikethat
                                            Jesus

he was a handsome man
                        and what i want to know is
how do you like your blueeyed boy
Mister Death

524 *'may my heart always'* .

may my heart always be open to little
birds who are the secrets of living
whatever they sing is better than to know
and if men should not hear them men are old

may my mind stroll about hungry
and fearless and thirsty and supple
and even if it's sunday may i be wrong
for whenever men are right they are not young

and may myself do nothing usefully
and love yourself so more than truly
there's never been quite such a fool who could fail
pulling all the sky over him with one smile

525 *'no time ago'*

no time ago
or else a life
walking in the dark
i met christ

jesus) my heart
flopped over
and lay still
while he passed (as

close as i'm to you
yes closer
made of nothing
except loneliness

526   *'Me up at does'*

Me up at does

out of the floor
quietly Stare

a poisoned mouse

still who alive

is asking What
have i done that

You wouldn't have

MARK VAN DOREN
1894–1972

527   *Good Appetite*

Of breakfast, then of walking to the pond;
Of wind, work, rain, and sleep I never tire.
God of monotony, may you be fond
Of me and these forever, and wood fire.

ROBERT GRAVES
1895–

528   *Flying Crooked*

The butterfly, a cabbage-white,
(His honest idiocy of flight)
Will never now, it is too late,
Master the art of flying straight,
Yet has—who knows so well as I?—
A just sense of how not to fly:
He lurches here and here by guess
And God and hope and hopelessness.
Even the aerobatic swift
Has not his flying-crooked gift.

529

At First Sight

'Love at first sight,' some say, misnaming
Discovery of twinned helplessness
Against the huge tug of procreation.

But friendship at first sight? This also
Catches fiercely at the surprised heart
So that the cheek blanches and then blushes.

530

On Dwelling

Courtesies of good-morning and good-evening
From rustic lips fail as the town encroaches:
Soon nothing passes but the cold quick stare
Of eyes that see ghosts, yet too many for fear.

Here I too walk, silent myself, in wonder
At a town not mine though plainly coextensive
With mine, even in days coincident:
In mine I dwell, in theirs like them I haunt.

And the green country, should I turn again there?
My bumpkin neighbours loom even ghostlier:
Like trees they murmur or like blackbirds sing
Courtesies of good-morning and good-evening.

531

The Beach

Louder than gulls the little children scream
Whom fathers haul into the jovial foam;
But others fearlessly rush in, breast high,
Laughing the salty water from their mouths—
Heroes of the nursery.

The horny boatman, who has seen whales
And flying fishes, who has sailed as far
As Demerara and the Ivory Coast,
Will warn them, when they crowd to hear his tales,
That every ocean smells alike of tar.

532 ## *Cat-Goddesses*

A perverse habit of cat-goddesses—
Even the blackest of them, black as coals
Save for a new moon blazing on each breast,
With coral tongues and beryl eyes like lamps,
Long-leggèd, pacing three by three in nines—
This obstinate habit is to yield themselves,
In verisimilar love-ecstasies,
To tatter-eared and slinking alley-toms
No less below the common run of cats
Than they above it; which they do for spite,
To provoke jealousy—not the least abashed
By such gross-headed, rabbit-coloured litters
As soon they shall be happy to desert.

533 ## *In Her Only Way*

When her need for you dies
    And she wanders apart,
Never rhetoricize
    On the faithless heart,

But with manlier virtue
    Be content to say
She both loved you and hurt you
    In her only way.

534 ## *She Is No Liar*

She is no liar, yet she will wash away
Honey from her lips, blood from her shadowy hand,
And, dressed at dawn in clean white robes will say,
Trusting the ignorant world to understand:
'Such things no longer are; this is today.'

535 *In Perspective*

What, keep love in *perspective?*—that old lie
Forced on the Imagination by the Eye
Which, mechanistically controlled, will tell
How rarely table-sides run parallel;
How distance shortens us; how wheels are found
Oval in shape far oftener than round;
How every ceiling-corner's out of joint;
How the broad highway tapers to a point—
Can all this fool us lovers? Not for long:
Even the blind will sense that something's wrong.

EDMUND BLUNDEN
1896–1974

536 *Departure*

The beech leaves caught in a moment gust
Run like bowled pennies in the autumn's dust
    And topple; frost like rain
Comes spangling down; through the prismy trees
Phœbus mistakes our horse for his,
    Such glory clothes his mane.

The stream makes his glen music alone
And plays upon shell and pot and stone—
    Our life's after-refrain;
Till in the sky the tower's old song
Reads us the hour, and reads it wrong,
And carter-like comes whistling along
    Our casual Anglian train.

HART CRANE
1899–1932

537   *Black Tambourine*

The interests of a black man in a cellar
Mark tardy judgment on the world's closed door.
Gnats toss in the shadow of a bottle,
And a roach spans a crevice in the floor.

Aesop, driven to pondering, found
Heaven with the tortoise and the hare;
Fox brush and sow ear top his grave
And mingling incantations on the air.

The black man, forlorn in the cellar,
Wanders in some mid-kingdom, dark, that lies,
Between his tambourine, stuck on the wall,
And, in Africa, a carcass quick with flies.

ROBERT FRANCIS
1901–

538   *Pitcher*

His art is eccentricity, his aim
How not to hit the mark he seems to aim at,

His passion how to avoid the obvious,
His technique how to vary the avoidance.

The others throw to be comprehended. He
Throws to be a moment misunderstood.

Yet not too much. Not errant, arrant, wild,
But every seeming aberration willed.

Not to, yet still, still to communicate
Making the batter understand too late.

ROY CAMPBELL

1902–1957

539   *Fishing Boats in Martigues*

Around the quays, kicked off in twos
The Four Winds dry their wooden shoes.

PATRICK MACDONOGH

1902–1961

540   *No Mean City*

Though naughty flesh will multiply
Our chief delight is in division;
Whatever of Divinity
We are all Doctors of Derision.
Content to risk a far salvation
For the quick coinage of a laugh
We cut, to make wit's reputation,
Our total of two friends by half.

A. S. J. TESSIMOND

1902–1962

541   *Postscript to a Pettiness*

Though you'll forgive, I think, my sweet,
My larger sins of haste and heat
And lust and fear, can you forgive
My inabilities to live?
Can you despise me not too much
When most I lack the human touch?
Promise to keep no diary of
Days when I fail, dear love, to love!

STEVIE SMITH

1902–1971

542   *The Murderer*

My true love breathed her latest breath
And I have closed her eyes in death.
It was a cold and windy day
In March, when my love went away.
She was not like other girls—rather diffident,
And that is how we had an accident.

543   *The Lads of the Village*

The lads of the village, we read in the lay,
By medalled commanders are muddled away,
And the picture that the poet makes is not very gay.

Poet, let the red blood flow, it makes the pattern better,
And let the tears flow, too, and grief stand that is their begetter,
And let man have his self-forged chain and hug every fetter.

For without the juxtaposition of muddles, medals and clay,
Would the picture be so very much more gay,
Would it not be a frivolous dance upon a summer's day?

Oh sing no more: Away with the folly of commanders.
This will not make a better song upon the field of Flanders,
Or upon any field of experience where pain makes patterns
  the poet slanders.

544 *Love Me!*

Love me, Love me, I cried to the rocks and the trees,
And Love me, they cried again, but it was only to tease.
Once I cried Love me to the people, but they fled like a dream,
And when I cried Love me to my friend, she began to scream.
Oh why do they leave me, the beautiful people, and only the
    rocks remain,
To cry Love me, as I cry Love me, and Love me again.

On the rock a baked sea-serpent lies,
And his eyelids close tightly over his violent eyes,
And I fear that his eyes will open and confound me with a
    mirthless word,
That the rocks will harp on for ever, and my Love me never be
    heard.

545 *Lady 'Rogue' Singleton*

Come, wed me, Lady Singleton,
And we will have a baby soon
And we will live in Edmonton
Where all the friendly people run.

I could never make you happy, darling,
Or give you the baby you want,
I would always very much rather, dear,
Live in a tent.

I am not a cold woman, Henry,
But I do not feel for you,
What I feel for the elephants and the miasmas
And the general view.

C. DAY LEWIS
1904–1972

546   *Where Are the War Poets?*

They who in folly or mere greed
Enslaved religion, markets, laws,
Borrow our language now and bid
Us to speak up in freedom's cause.

It is the logic of our times,
No subject for immortal verse—
That we who lived by honest dreams
Defend the bad against the worse.

RICHARD EBERHART
1904–

547   *For a Lamb*

I saw on the slant hill a putrid lamb,
Propped with daisies. The sleep looked deep.
The face nudged in the green pillow
But the guts were out for crows to eat.

Where's the lamb? whose tender plaint
Said all for the mute breezes.
Say he's in the wind somewhere,
Say, there's a lamb in the daisies.

NORMAN CAMERON

1905–1953

548

She and I

She and I, we thought and fought
And each of us won by the other's defeat;
She and I, we danced and pranced
And lost by neglect the use of our feet;
She and I caught ills and chills
And were cured or dead before we could cough;
She and I, we walked and talked
Half an hour after our heads were cut off.

549

The Compassionate Fool

My enemy had bidden me as guest.
His table all set out with wine and cake,
His ordered chairs, he to beguile me dressed
So neatly, moved my pity for his sake.

I knew it was an ambush, but could not
Leave him to eat his cake up by himself
And put his unused glasses on the shelf.
I made pretence of falling in his plot,

And trembled when in his anxiety
He bared it too absurdly to my view.
And even as he stabbed me through and through
I pitied him for his small strategy.

550

Forgive Me, Sire

Forgive me, Sire, for cheating your intent,
That I, who should command a regiment,
Do amble amiably here, O God,
One of the neat ones in your awkward squad.

225

551   *Shepherdess*

All day my sheep have mingled with yours. They strayed
Into your valley seeking a change of ground.
Held and bemused with what they and I had found,
Pastures and wonders, heedlessly I delayed.

Now it is late. The tracks leading home are steep,
The stars and landmarks in your country are strange.
How can I take my sheep back over the range?
Shepherdess, show me now where I may sleep.

PHYLLIS McGINLEY

1905–1978

552   *The Temptations of Saint Anthony*

Off in the wilderness bare and level,
Anthony wrestled with the Devil.
Once he'd beaten the Devil down,
Anthony'd turn his eyes toward town
And leave his hermitage now and then
To come to grips with the souls of men.

Afterward, all the tales agree,
Wrestling the Devil seemed to be
Quite a relief to Anthony.

553   *The Adversary*

A mother's hardest to forgive.
Life is the fruit she longs to hand you,
Ripe on a plate. And while you live,
Relentlessly she understands you.

226

PHYLLIS MCGINLEY

Trinity Place

554

The pigeons that peck at the grass in Trinity Churchyard
  Are pompous as bankers. They walk with an air, they preen
Their prosperous feathers. They smugly regard their beauty.
  They are plump, they are sleek. It is only the men who are
    lean.

The pigeons scan with disfavor the men who sit there,
  Listless in sun or shade. The pigeons sidle
Between the gravestones with shrewd, industrious motions.
  The pigeons are busy. It is only the men who are idle.

The pigeons sharpen their beaks on the stones, and they waddle
  In dignified search of their proper, their daily bread.
Their eyes are small with contempt for the men on the benches.
  It is only the men who are hungry. The pigeons are fed.

PATRICK KAVANAGH
1906–1967

555   *Leave Them Alone*

There's nothing happening that you hate
That's really worthwhile slamming;
Be patient. If you only wait
You'll see time gently damning

Newspaper bedlamites who raised
Each day the devil's howl,
Versifiers who had seized
The poet's begging bowl;

The whole hysterical passing show
The hour apotheosised
Into a cul-de-sac will go
And be not even despised.

227

VERNON WATKINS
1906–1967

556   *Old Triton Time*

Old Triton Time responds to every mood:
He's the newborn who's older than the flood.
He babbles water from a dull stone tongue.
He's old and cold, and yet the water's young.
To gain him is to lose him. I have seen
Loss bind him up with lichens: he grew green.
But if my fingers touch the water cold,
He suddenly seems young, the water old.

SAMUEL BECKETT
1906–

557   *Gnome*

Spend the years of learning squandering
Courage for the years of wandering
Through a world politely turning
From the loutishness of learning.

JOHN BETJEMAN
1906–1984

558   *Death of King George V*

'New King arrives in his capital by air . . .' Daily Newspaper

Spirits of well-shot woodcock, partridge, snipe
Flutter and bear him up the Norfolk sky:
In that red house in a red mahogany book-case
The stamp collection waits with mounts long dry.

228

The big blue eyes are shut which saw wrong clothing
   And favourite fields and coverts from a horse;
Old men in country houses hear clocks ticking
   Over thick carpets with a deadened force;

Old men who never cheated, never doubted,
   Communicated monthly, sit and stare
At the new suburb stretched beyond the run-way
   Where a young man lands hatless from the air.

559   *Remorse*

The lungs draw in the air and rattle it out again;
   The eyes revolve in their sockets and upwards stare;
No more worry and waiting and troublesome doubt again—
   She whom I loved and left is no longer there.

The nurse puts down her knitting and walks across to her,
   With quick professional eye she surveys the dead.
Just one patient the less and little the loss to her,
   Distantly tender she settles the shrunken head.

Protestant claims and Catholic, the wrong and the right
      of them,
   Unimportant they seem in the face of death—
But my neglect and unkindness—to lose the sight of them
   I would listen even again to that labouring breath.

WILLIAM EMPSON
1906–1984

560   *Let It Go*

It is this deep blankness is the real thing strange.
   The more things happen to you the more you can't
   Tell or remember even what they were.

The contradictions cover such a range.
The talk would talk and go so far aslant.
You don't want madhouse and the whole thing there.

LOUIS MacNEICE
1907–1963

561 *Snow*

The room was suddenly rich and the great bay-window was
Spawning snow and pink roses against it
Soundlessly collateral and incompatible:
World is suddener than we fancy it.

World is crazier and more of it than we think,
Incorrigibly plural. I peel and portion
A tangerine and spit the pips and feel
The drunkenness of things being various.

And the fire flames with a bubbling sound for world
Is more spiteful and gay than one supposes—
On the tongue on the eyes on the ears in the palms of one's
  hands—
There is more than glass between the snow and the huge roses.

562 *The Ear*

There are many sounds which are neither music nor voice,
There are many visitors in masks or in black glasses
Climbing the spiral staircase of the ear. The choice
Of callers is not ours. Behind the hedge
Of night they wait to pounce. A train passes,
The thin and audible end of a dark wedge.

We should like to lie alone in a deaf hollow
Cocoon of self where no person or thing would speak:
In fact we lie and listen as a man might follow
A will o' the wisp in an endless eyeless bog,
Follow the terrible drone of a cockchafer, or the bleak
Oracle of a barking dog.

563 *Night Club*

After the legshows and the brandies
And all the pick-me-ups for tired
Men there is a feeling
Something more is required.

The lights go down and eyes
Look up across the room;
Salome comes in, bearing
The head of God knows whom.

564 *Precursors*

O that the rain would come—the rain in big battalions—
Or thunder flush the hedge a more clairvoyant green
Or wind walk in and whip us and strip us or booming
Harvest moon transmute this muted scene.

But all is flat, matt, mute, unlivened, unexpectant,
And none but insects dare to sing or pirouette;
That Man is a dancer is an anachronism—
Who has forgotten his steps or hardly learnt them yet.

Yet one or two we have known who had the gusto
Of wind or water-spout, and one or two
Who carry an emerald lamp behind their faces
And—during thunder-storms—the light comes shining
    through.

565 *Figure of Eight*

In the top and front of a bus, eager to meet his fate,
He pressed with foot and mind to gather speed,
Then, when the lights were changing, jumped and hurried,
Though dead on time, to the meeting place agreed,
But there was no one there. He chose to wait.
No one came. He need not perhaps have worried.

Whereas today in the rear and gloom of a train,
Loath, loath to meet his fate, he cowers and prays
For some last-minute hitch, some unheard-of abdication,
But, winding up the black thread of his days,
The wheels roll on and make it all too plain
Who will be there to meet him at the station.

W. H. AUDEN

1907–1973

566 *Gare du Midi*

A nondescript express in from the South,
Crowds round the ticket barrier, a face
To welcome which the mayor has not contrived
Bugles or braid: something about the mouth
Distracts the stray look with alarm and pity.
Snow is falling. Clutching a little case,
He walks out briskly to infect a city
Whose terrible future may have just arrived.

567 *Epitaph on a Tyrant*

Perfection, of a kind, was what he was after,
And the poetry he invented was easy to understand;
He knew human folly like the back of his hand,
And was greatly interested in armies and fleets;
When he laughed, respectable senators burst with laughter,
And when he cried the little children died in the streets.

568   *'Base words are uttered'*

Base words are uttered only by the base
And can for such at once be understood,
But noble platitudes:—ah, there's a case
Where the most careful scrutiny is needed
To tell a voice that's genuinely good
From one that's base but merely has succeeded.

569   *'Behold the manly mesomorph'*

Behold the manly mesomorph
Showing his bulging biceps off,
Whom social workers love to touch,
Though the loveliest girls do not care for him much.

Pretty to watch with bat or ball,
An Achilles, too, in a bar-room brawl,
But in the ditch of hopeless odds,
The hour of desertion by brass and gods,

Not a hero. It is the pink-and-white,
Fastidious, almost girlish, in the night
When the proud-arsed broad-shouldered break and run,
Who covers their retreat, dies at his gun.

570   *At the Party*

Unrhymed, unrhythmical, the chatter goes:
Yet no one hears his own remarks as prose.

Beneath each topic tunelessly discussed
The ground-bass is reciprocal mistrust.

The names in fashion shuttling to and fro
Yield, when deciphered, messages of woe.

You cannot read me like an open book.
I'm more myself than you will ever look.

233

Will no one listen to my little song?
Perhaps I shan't be with you very long.

A howl for recognition, shrill with fear,
Shakes the jam-packed apartment, but each ear
Is listening to its hearing, so none hear.

571 ## *August 1968*

The Ogre does what ogres can,
Deeds quite impossible for Man,
But one prize is beyond his reach,
The Ogre cannot master Speech.
About a subjugated plain,
Among its desperate and slain,
The Ogre stalks with hands on hips,
While drivel gushes from his lips.

A. D. HOPE
1907–

572 ## *The Bed*

The doctor loves the patient,
The patient loves his bed;
A fine place to be born in,
The best place to be dead.

The doctor loves the patient
Because he means to die;
The patient loves the patient bed
That shares his agony.

The bed adores the doctor,
His cool and skilful touch
Soon brings another patient
Who loves her just as much.

THEODORE ROETHKE
1908–1963

573   *Old Florist*

That hump of a man bunching chrysanthemums
Or pinching-back asters, or planting azaleas,
Tamping and stamping dirt into pots,—
How he could flick and pick
Rotten leaves or yellowy petals,
Or scoop out a weed close to flourishing roots,
Or make the dust buzz with a light spray,
Or drown a bug in one spit of tobacco juice,
Or fan life into wilted sweet-peas with his hat,
Or stand all night watering roses, his feet blue in rubber boots.

574   *Dolor*

I have known the inexorable sadness of pencils,
Neat in their boxes, dolor of pad and paper-weight,
All the misery of manilla folders and mucilage,
Desolation in immaculate public places,
Lonely reception room, lavatory, switchboard,
The unalterable pathos of basin and pitcher,
Ritual of multigraph, paper-clip, comma,
Endless duplication of lives and objects.
And I have seen dust from the walls of institutions,
Finer than flour, alive, more dangerous than silica,
Sift, almost invisible, through long afternoons of tedium,
Dropping a fine film on nails and delicate eyebrows,
Glazing the pale hair, the duplicate grey standard faces.

575 *Night Crow*

When I saw that clumsy crow
Flap from a wasted tree,
A shape in the mind rose up:
Over the gulfs of dream
Flew a tremendous bird
Further and further away
Into a moonless black,
Deep in the brain, far back.

576 *Wish for a Young Wife*

My lizard, my lively writher,
May your limbs never wither,
May the eyes in your face
Survive the green ice
Of envy's mean gaze;
May you live out your life
Without hate, without grief,
And your hair ever blaze,
In the sun, in the sun,
When I am undone,
When I am no one.

W. R. RODGERS
1909–1969

577 *Words*

Always the arriving winds of words
Pour like Atlantic gales over these ears,
These reefs, these foils and fenders, these shrinking
And sea-scalded edges of the brain-land.
Rebutted and rebounding, on they post
Past my remembrance, falling all unplanned.
But some day out of darkness they'll come forth,
Arrowed and narrowed into my tongue's tip,
And speak for me—their most astonished host.

W. R. RODGERS

578   *War-Time*

Now all our hurries that hung up on hooks,
And all our heels that idly kicked in halls,
And all our angers that at anchor swung,
And all our youth long tethered to dole-lines,
And all our roots that rotted deep in dump,
Are recollected: in country places
Old men gather the children round them now,
As an old tree, when lopped of every bough,
Gathers the young leaves into itself, a frilled stump.

579   *The Lovers*

After the tiff there was stiff silence, till
One word, flung in centre like single stone,
Starred and cracked the ice of her resentment
To its edge. From that stung core opened and
Poured up one outward and widening wave
Of eager and extravagant anger.

JAMES REEVES
1909–1978

580   *The Stone Gentleman*

Let us move the stone gentleman to the toadstool wood:
Too long has he disapproved in our market-place.
Within the manifold stone creases of his frock-coat
   Let the woodlouse harbour and thrive.

Let the hamadryads wreath him with bryony,
The scrolled fern-fronds greenly fantasticate,
And sappy etiolations cluster damply
   About the paternal knee.

Them the abrupt, blank eyes will not offend.
The civic brow and raised, suppressive hand
Unchallenged and without affront shall manage
   The republic of tall spiders.

581   *The Double Autumn*

Better to close the book and say good-night
When nothing moves you much but your own plight.
Neither the owl's noise through the dying grove
Where the small creatures insecurely move,
Nor what the moon does to the huddled trees,
Nor the admission that such things as these
Would have excited once can now excite.
Better close down the double autumn night
Than practise dumbly staring at your plight.

582   *Things to Come*

The shadow of a fat man in the moonlight
   Precedes me on the road down which I go;
And should I turn and run, he would pursue me:
   This is the man whom I must get to know.

ROBERT FITZGERALD

1910–1985

583   *Entreaty*

Summer come soon and turn the sickness from my house,
which from sour early darkness, damp wind, spiteful rain,
took shelter beside our fire, and through these months has lain
like a tame cat on the beds or crept up like a mouse,

or stood at doorways like a stranger's unwanted dog,
mangy and treacherous—ill comrade to be found
at play with children. . . . So the comfortless time goes round;
and evening coughs cold air and dawn is phlegmed with fog.

Until it seems we must be utterly dispossessed,
unless on the world's shoulders that swing with the poles and
  dip
summer come cantering south to crack the sun, his whip,
about the lean hindquarters of my yelping, unpleasant guest.

NORMAN MacCAIG

1910–

584   *Stars and Planets*

Trees are cages for them: water holds its breath
To balance them without smudging on its delicate meniscus.
Children watch them playing in their heavenly playground;
Men use them to lug ships across oceans, through firths.

They seem so twinkle-still, but they never cease
Inventing new spaces and huge explosions
And migrating in mathematical tribes over
The steppes of space at their outrageous ease.

It's hard to think that the earth is one—
This poor sad bearer of wars and disasters
Rolls-Roycing round the sun with its load of gangsters,
Attended only by the loveless moon.

ELIZABETH BISHOP

1911–1979

585   Casabianca

Love's the boy stood on the burning deck
trying to recite 'The boy stood on
the burning deck'. Love's the son
  stood stammering elocution
  while the poor ship in flames went down.

Love's the obstinate boy, the ship,
even the swimming sailors, who
would like a schoolroom platform, too,
   or an excuse to stay
  on deck. And love's the burning boy.

J. V. CUNNINGHAM
1911–

586   *In Innocence*

In innocence I said,
'Affection is secure.
It is not forced or led.'
No longer sure

Of the least certainty
I have erased the mind,
As mendicants who see
Mimic the blind.

587   *'I had gone broke'*

I had gone broke, and got set to come back,
And lost, on a hot day and a fast track,
On a long shot at long odds, a black mare
By Hatred out of Envy by Despair.

588   *Interview with Doctor Drink*

I have a fifth of therapy
In the house, and transference there.
Doctor, there's not much wrong with me,
Only a sick rattlesnake somewhere

J. V. CUNNINGHAM

In the house, if it be there at all,
But the lithe mouth is coiled. The shapes
Of door and window move. I call.
What is it that pulls down the drapes,

Disheveled and exposed? Your rye
Twists in my throat: intimacy
Is like hard liquor. Who but I
Coil there and squat, and pay your fee?

ROY FULLER

1912–

589   *During a Bombardment by V-Weapons*

The little noises of the house:
Drippings between the slates and ceiling;
From the electric fire's cooling,
Tickings; the dry feet of a mouse:

These at the ending of a war
Have power to alarm me more
Than the ridiculous detonations
Outside the gently coughing curtains.

And, love, I see your pallor bears
A far more pointed threat than steel.
Now all the permanent and real
Furies are settling in upstairs.

590   *Memorial Poem*

N.S. 1888–1949
Illness is to reconcile us to death

Week after week, month after month, in pain
You wrestled with that fiendish enemy—
The thing that tried in vain
To drag you from the room to its own territory.

241

ROY FULLER

Each day renewed the duel and our grief
Until at last upon the crumpled bed—
To our unwished relief—
The strange emaciated brown-faced fiend lay dead.

591   *The Hittites*

Short, big-nosed men with nasty conical caps,
Occasionally leering but mostly glum,
Retroussé shoes and swords at oblong hips—

Or so the stone reliefs depicted them.
But how trustworthy can those pictures be?
Even in that remote millennium

The artist must have seen society
From some idiosyncratic vantage point.
Short, big-nosed, glum, no doubt, but cowardly,

For him, as always, the time was out of joint;
And his great patrons as they passed the stone
Would turn their eyes and mutter that complaint

Whose precise nature never will be known.

F. T. PRINCE

1912–

592   *The Wind in the Tree*

She has decided that she no longer loves me.
There is nothing to be done. I long ago
As a child thought the tree sighed 'Do I know
Whether my motion makes the wind that moves me?'

242

GEORGE BARKER

1913–

593   *'The village coddled in the valley'*

The village coddled in the valley,
The bird cuddled in the cloud,
The small fish nested, the babe breasted,
Sleep with a deeper dream endowed:
For them this evening especially
Hangs its veils over all the world.

Whickering child and weeping lamb
Interchange in the general care
That Nature, cradling kind in her arm,
Extends to all new things that are:
As, walking clouds, she keeps from harm
The whickering child and weeping lamb.

594   *Epitaph for the Poet*

The single sleeper lying here
    Is neither lying nor asleep.
Bend down your nosey parker ear
    And eavesdrop on him. In the deep
Conundrum of the dirt he speaks
    The one word you will never hear.

595   *'Not in the poet'*

Not in the poet is the poem or
even the poetry. It is hiding behind
a broken wall or a geranium
or walking around pretending to be blind
seeking a home that it cannot find.

Into the ego that has emptied out
everything except its abstract being
and left only a shell, the poem then
moves silently, foreseeing
its purpose is to haunt the shell like singing.

R. S. THOMAS
1913–

596 *Ire*

Are you out, woman of the lean pelt,
And the table unlaid and bare
As a boar's backside, and the kettle
Loud as an old man, plagued with spittle,
Or a cat fight upon the stair?
The sink stinks, and the floor unscrubbed
Is no mirror for the preening sun
At the cracked lattice. Oh, the oven's cold
As Jesus' church, and never a bun
Lurks in the larder—Is this the way
You welcome your man from his long mowing
Of the harsh, unmannerly, mountain hay?

DYLAN THOMAS
1914–1953

597 *'On no work of words'*

On no work of words now for three lean months in the
    bloody
Belly of the rich year and the big purse of my body
I bitterly take to task my poverty and craft:

To take to give is all, return what is hungrily given
Puffing the pounds of manna up through the dew to heaven,
The lovely gift of the gab bangs back on a blind shaft.

To lift to leave from the treasures of man is pleasing death
That will rake at last all currencies of the marked breath
And count the taken, forsaken mysteries in a bad dark.

To surrender now is to pay the expensive ogre twice.
Ancient woods of my blood, dash down to the nut of the seas
If I take to burn or return this world which is each man's
    work.

598   *Twenty-Four Years*

Twenty-four years remind the tears of my eyes.
(Bury the dead for fear that they walk to the grave in labour.)
In the groin of the natural doorway I crouched like a tailor
Sewing a shroud for a journey
By the light of the meat-eating sun.
Dressed to die, the sensual strut begun,
With my red veins full of money,
In the final direction of the elementary town
I advance for as long as forever is.

RANDALL JARRELL
1914–1965

599   *The Death of the Ball Turret Gunner*

From my mother's sleep I fell into the State,
And I hunched in its belly till my wet fur froze.
Six miles from earth, loosed from its dream of life,
I woke to black flak and the nightmare fighters.
When I died they washed me out of the turret with a hose.

600   *A War*

There set out, slowly, for a Different World,
At four, on winter mornings, different legs . . .
You can't break eggs without making an omelette
—That's what they tell the eggs.

RANDALL JARRELL

601 *Well Water*

What a girl called 'the dailiness of life'
(Adding an errand to your errand. Saying,
'Since you're up ...' Making you a means to
A means to a means to) is well water
Pumped from an old well at the bottom of the world.
The pump you pump the water from is rusty
And hard to move and absurd, a squirrel-wheel
A sick squirrel turns slowly, through the sunny
Inexorable hours. And yet sometimes
The wheel turns of its own weight, the rusty
Pump pumps over your sweating face the clear
Water, cold, so cold! you cup your hands
And gulp from them the dailiness of life.

CLIFFORD DYMENT

1914–1971

602 *Fox*

Exploiter of the shadows
He moved among the fences,
A strip of action coiling
Around his farmyard fancies.

With shouting fields are shaken,
The spinneys give no shelter;
There is delight for riders,
For hounds a tooth in shoulder.

The creature tense with wildness
Knows death is sudden falling
From fury into weary
Surrendering of feeling.

246

JOHN BERRYMAN

1914–1972

603   *He Resigns*

Age, and the deaths, and the ghosts.
Her having gone away
in spirit from me. Hosts
of regrets come & find me empty.

I don't feel this will change.
I don't want any thing
or person, familiar or strange.
I don't think I will sing

any more just now,
or ever. I must start
to sit with a blind brow
above an empty heart.

604   *King David Dances*

Aware to the dry throat of the wide hell in the world,
O trampling empires, and mine one of them,
and mine one gross desire against His sight,
slaughter devising there,
some good behind, ambiguous ahead,
revolted sons, a pierced son, bound to bear,
mid hypocrites amongst idolaters,
mockt in abysm by one shallow wife,
with the ponder both of priesthood & of State
heavy upon me, yea,
all the black same I dance my blue head off!

247

NORMAN NICHOLSON
1914–1982

605 *Weather Ear*

Lying in bed in the dark, I hear the bray
Of the furnace hooter rasping the slates, and say:
'The wind will be in the east, and frost on the nose, today.'

Or when, in the still, small, conscience hours, I hear
The market clock-bell clacking close to my ear:
'A north-west wind from the fell, and the sky-light swilled and
    clear.'

But now when the roofs are sulky as the dead,
With a snuffle and sniff in the gullies, a drip on the lead:
'No wind at all, and the street stone-deaf with a cold in the
    head.'

LAURIE LEE
1914–

606 *Invasion Summer*

The evening, the heather,
the unsecretive cuckoo
and butterflies in their disorder,
not a word of war as we lie
our mouths in a hot nest
and the flowers advancing.

Does a hill defend itself,
does a river run to earth
to hide its quaint neutrality?
A boy is shot with England in his brain,
but she lies brazen yet beneath the sun,
she has no honour and she has no fear.

248

C. H. SISSON

1914–

607   *Money*

I was led into captivity by the bitch business
Not in love but in what seemed a physical necessity
And now I cannot even watch the spring
The itch for subsistence having become responsibility.

Money the she-devil comes to us under many veils
Tactful at first, calling herself beauty.
Tear away this disguise, she proposes paternal solicitude
Assuming the dishonest face of duty.

Suddenly you are in bed with a screeching tear-sheet.
This is money at last without her night-dress
Clutching you against her fallen udders and sharp bones
In an unscrupulous and deserved embrace.

608   *Easter*

One good crucifixion and he rose from the dead
He knew better than to wait for age
To nibble his intellect
And depress his love.

Out in the desert the sun beats and the cactus
Prickles more fiercely than any in his wilderness
And his forty days
Were merely monastic.

What he did on the cross was no more
Than others have done for less reason
And the resurrection you could take for granted.

What is astonishing is that he came here at all
Where no one ever came voluntarily before.

249

JUDITH WRIGHT

1915–

609 *Portrait*

It was a heartfelt game, when it began—
polish and cook and sew and mend, contrive,
move between sink and stove, keep flower-beds weeded—
all her love needed was that it was needed,
and merely living kept the blood alive.

Now an old habit leads from sink to stove,
mends and keeps clean the house that looks like home,
and waits in hunger dressed to look like love
for the calm return of those who, when they come,
remind her: this was a game, when it began.

THOMAS BLACKBURN

1916–1977

610 *Families*

Children who love more than they hate
Parents from whom their birthdays date,
Can be apart without excuses;
Sharing the heart's abiding places.
But those who hate more than they love
Are often fated like a slave
To live in foul, domestic weather
Since hate keeps enemies together.
I see no ending to such plight
Except my usual; more insight.

JOHN CIARDI
1916–

611   *Plea*

I said to her tears: 'I am fallible and hungry,
and refusal is no correction and anger no meal.
Feed me mercies from the first-bread of your heart.

I have invented no part of the error it is
to be human. The least law could jail me
and be upheld; the least theology, damn me

and be proved. But when, ever, have I come to you
to be judged? Set me straight to your last breath,
and mine, and feed me most what I need not deserve

—or starve yourself, and starve me, and be right.'

GAVIN EWART
1916–

612   *Ending*

The love we thought would never stop
now cools like a congealing chop.
The kisses that were hot as curry
are bird-pecks taken in a hurry.
The hands that held electric charges
now lie inert as four moored barges.
The feet that ran to meet a date
are running slow and running late.
The eyes that shone and seldom shut
are victims of a power cut.
The parts that then transmitted joy
are now reserved and cold and coy.
Romance, expected once to stay,
has left a note saying GONE AWAY.

251

613   *A 14-Year-Old Convalescent Cat in the Winter*

I want him to have another living summer,
to lie in the sun and enjoy the *douceur de vivre*—
because the sun, like golden rum in a rummer,
is what makes an idle cat *un tout petit peu ivre*—

I want him to lie stretched out, contented,
revelling in the heat, his fur all dry and warm,
an Old Age Pensioner, retired, resented
by no one, and happinesses in a beelike swarm

to settle on him—postponed for another season
that last fated hateful journey to the vet
from which there is no return (and age the reason),
which must soon come—as I cannot forget.

ROBERT LOWELL

1917–1977

614   *Lady Ralegh's Lament*

1618

Sir Walter, oh, oh, my own Sir Walter—
the sour Tower and the Virgin Queen's garden close
are deflowered and gone now . . .
Horrible the connoisseur tyrant's querulous strut;
an acorn dances in a girdle of green oak leaves
up the steps to the scaffold to the block,
square bastard of an oak. Clearly, clearly,
the Atlantic whitens to merge Sir Walter's head,
still dangling in its scarlet, tangled twine,
as if beseeching voyage. Voyage?
Down and down; the compass needle dead on terror.

WILLIAM JAY SMITH
1918–

615   *American Primitive*

Look at him there in his stovepipe hat,
His high-top shoes, and his handsome collar;
Only my Daddy could look like that,
And I love my Daddy like he loves his Dollar.

The screen door bangs, and it sounds so funny—
There he is in a shower of gold;
His pockets are stuffed with folding money,
His lips are blue, and his hands feel cold.

He hangs in the hall by his black cravat,
The ladies faint, and the children holler:
Only my Daddy could look like that,
And I love my Daddy like he loves his Dollar.

MURIEL SPARK
1918–

616   *Faith and Works*

My friend is always doing Good
But doubts the Meaning of his labour,
While I by Faith am much imbued
And can't be bothered with my Neighbour.

These mortal heresies in us
Friendship makes orthodox and thus
We are the truest Saints alive
As near as two and two make five.

WILLIAM MEREDITH

1919–

617 *Iambic Feet Considered as Honorable Scars*

You see these little scars? That's where my wife
—The principle of order everywhere—
Grazes me, shooting at the sloppy bear
That lurches from the urinals of life.
He is the principle of god knows what;
He wants things to be shapeless and all hair.
Only a fool would want to fight him fair,
Only a woman would think he could be shot.

D. J. ENRIGHT

1920–

618 *The Monuments of Hiroshima*

The roughly estimated ones, who do not sort well
    with our common phrases,
Who are by no means eating roots of dandelion,
    or pushing up the daisies.

The more or less anonymous, to whom no human idiom
    can apply,
Who neither passed away, or on,
    nor went before, nor vanished on a sigh.

Little of peace for them to rest in, less of them
    to rest in peace:
Dust to dust a swift transition, ashes to ash
    with awful ease.

Their only monument will be of others' casting—
A Tower of Peace, a Hall of Peace, a Bridge of Peace
    —who might have wished for something lasting,
Like a wooden box.

619 *Development*

The house of God is due to be converted.
These days He has no need of so much space,
The children all grown up and moved away.
A family scattered, sad but commonplace.

Bowling or housey-housey? No theatre
Or other devil's playground, heaven forfend!
A last stroll round the old backyard, and then
He leaves to room with some old Reverend.

HOWARD NEMEROV

1920–

620 *An Old Picture*

Two children, dressed in court costume,
Go hand in hand through a rich room.
He bears a scepter, she a book;
Their eyes exchange a serious look.

High in a gallery above,
Grave persons frown upon their love;
Yonder behind the silken screen
Whispers the bishop with the queen.

These hold the future tightly reined,
It shall be as they have ordained;
The bridal bed already made,
The crypt also richly arrayed.

621 *A Negro Cemetery Next to a White One*

I wouldn't much object, if I were black,
To being turned away at the iron gate
By the dark blonde angel holding up a plaque
That said White only; who would mind the wait

For those facilities? And still it's odd,
Though a natural god-given civil right,
For men to throw it in the face of God
Some ghosts are black and some darknesses white.

But since they failed to integrate the earth,
It's white of them to give what tantamounts
To it, making us all, for what that's worth,
Separate but equal where it counts.

622 *The Death of God*

The celebrants came chanting 'God is dead!'
And all as one the nations bowed the head
Thanksgiving; knowing not how shrewdly the rod
Would bite the back in the kingdom of dead God.

623 *Casting*

The waters deep, the waters dark,
Reflect the seekers, hide the sought,
Whether in water or in air to drown.
Between them curls the silver spark,
Barbed, baited, waiting, of a thought—
Which in the world is upside down,
The fish hook or the question mark?

DRUMMOND ALLISON

1921–1943

624 *O Sheriffs*

O sheriffs hung with long pearlhandled guns
Showing your stars, coachditching dark road-agents,
O Pony Express on Sioux-surrounded plains.

Mushers of huskies, dudes in border towns,
Rustlers of painted mustangs down thin gorges
And tumblers out of rustler-run saloons.

O Darrell who the revolving logs defy,
O Billy caught with bacon, mad-eyed Hardin
Daring to draw each pallid deputy.

God like a lone and lemon-drinking Ranger,
Or at a far fur-station the half-breed stranger,
Them string up undecayed and stellify.

625   *King Lot's Envoys*

Oh! to have hidden in the undergrowth
With seven churls from any nasty nation
And seen the envoys in their bog-black livery
Make signs and start their cross-roads conversation!

Then to have used at last our homemade maces
And left them blind and legless and unsexed,
And living on King Lot's especial coinage,
Waited with ale and girls for what came next!

RICHARD WILBUR

1921–

626   *Epistemology*

I

Kick at the rock, Sam Johnson, break your bones:
But cloudy, cloudy is the stuff of stones.

II

We milk the cow of the world, and as we do
We whisper in her ear, 'You are not true.'

627 *Parable*

I read how Quixote in his random ride
Came to a crossing once, and lest he lose
The purity of chance, would not decide

Whither to fare, but wished his horse to choose.
For glory lay wherever he might turn.
His head was light with pride, his horse's shoes

Were heavy, and he headed for the barn.

628 *Piazza di Spagna, Early Morning*

      I can't forget
How she stood at the top of that long marble stair
  Amazed, and then with a sleepy pirouette
Went dancing slowly down to the fountain-quieted square;

      Nothing upon her face
But some impersonal loneliness,—not then a girl,
  But as it were a reverie of the place,
      A called-for falling glide and whirl;

  As when a leaf, petal, or thin chip
Is drawn to the falls of a pool and, circling a moment above
  it,
      Rides on over the lip—
Perfectly beautiful, perfectly ignorant of it.

629 *Mind*

Mind in its purest play is like some bat
That beats about in caverns all alone,
Contriving by a kind of senseless wit
Not to conclude against a wall of stone.

It has no need to falter or explore;
Darkly it knows what obstacles are there,
And so may weave and flitter, dip and soar
In perfect courses through the blackest air.

And has this simile a like perfection?
The mind is like a bat. Precisely. Save
That in the very happiest intellection
A graceful error may correct the cave.

630 *The Proof*

Shall I love God for causing me to be?
I was mere utterance; shall these words love me?

Yet when I caused his work to jar and stammer,
And one free subject loosened all his grammar,

I love him that he did not in a rage
Once and forever rule me off the page,

But, thinking I might come to please him yet,
Crossed out *delete* and wrote his patient *stet*.

ANTHONY HECHT

1922–

631 *Avarice*

The penniless Indian fakirs and their camels
    Slip through the needle's eye
To bliss (for neither flesh nor spirit trammels
    Such as are prone to die)
And from emaciate heaven they behold
    Our sinful kings confer
Upon an infant huge tributes of gold
    And frankincense and myrrh.

PHILIP LARKIN

1922–

632   *Home Is So Sad*

Home is so sad. It stays as it was left,
Shaped to the comfort of the last to go
As if to win them back. Instead, bereft
Of anyone to please, it withers so,
Having no heart to put aside the theft

And turn again to what it started as,
A joyous shot at how things ought to be,
Long fallen wide. You can see how it was:
Look at the pictures and the cutlery.
The music in the piano stool. That vase.

633   *Water*

If I were called in
To construct a religion
I should make use of water.

Going to church
Would entail a fording
To dry, different clothes;

My litany would employ
Images of sousing,
A furious devout drench,

And I should raise in the east
A glass of water
Where any-angled light
Would congregate endlessly.

634 *Days*

What are days for?
Days are where we live.
They come, they wake us
Time and time over.
They are to be happy in:
Where can we live but days?

Ah, solving that question
Brings the priest and the doctor
In their long coats
Running over the fields.

635 *As Bad as a Mile*

Watching the shied core
Striking the basket, skidding across the floor,
Shows less and less of luck, and more and more

Of failure spreading back up the arm
Earlier and earlier, the unraised hand calm,
The apple unbitten in the palm.

ALAN DUGAN

1923–

636 *Memories of Verdun*

The men laughed and baaed like sheep
and marched across the flashing day
to the flashing valley. A shaved
pig in a uniform led the way.

I crawled down Old Confusion, hid,
and groaned for years about my crime:
was I the proper coward, they
heroically wrong? I lived out their time!,

a hard labor, convict by look and word:
I was the fool and am penitent:
I was afraid of a nothing, a death;
they were afraid of less, its lieutenant.

ROBERT CREELEY
1926–

637   *I Know a Man*

As I sd to my
friend, because I am
always talking,—John, I

sd, which was not his
name, the darkness sur-
rounds us, what

can we do against
it, or else, shall we &
why not, buy a goddamn big car,

drive, he sd, for
christ's sake, look
out where yr going.

ELIZABETH JENNINGS
1926–

638   *Answers*

I kept my answers small and kept them near;
Big questions bruised my mind but still I let
Small answers be a bulwark to my fear.

The huge abstractions I kept from the light;
Small things I handled and caressed and loved.
I let the stars assume the whole of night.

But the big answers clamoured to be moved
Into my life. Their great audacity
Shouted to be acknowledged and believed.

Even when all small answers build up to
Protection of my spirit, still I hear
Big answers striving for their overthrow

And all the great conclusions coming near.

JAMES MERRILL

1926–

639   *A Renewal*

Having used every subterfuge
To shake you, lies, fatigue, or even that of passion,
Now I see no way but a clean break.
I add that I am willing to bear the guilt.

You nod assent. Autumn turns windy, huge,
A clear vase of dry leaves vibrating on and on.
We sit, watching. When I next speak
Love buries itself in me, up to the hilt.

GALWAY KINNELL
1927–

640   *In a Parlor Containing a Table*

In a parlor containing a table
And three chairs, three men confided
Their inmost thoughts to one another.
I, said the first, am miserable.
I am miserable, the second said.
I think that for me the correct word
Is miserable, asserted the third.
Well, they said at last, it's quarter to two.
Good night. Cheer up. Sleep well.
You too. You too. You too.

W. S. MERWIN
1927–

641   *When the War Is Over*

When the war is over
We will be proud of course the air will be
Good for breathing at last
The water will have been improved the salmon
And the silence of heaven will migrate more perfectly
The dead will think the living are worth it we will know
Who we are
And we will all enlist again.

JAMES MICHIE

1927–

642

To My Daughter

When I'm far out in drink, your musical box
Gives me the horrors. Mermaids on the rocks,
Beached rabbits, stranded starfish, teddy bears—
Simpering pyknic picnickers in pairs—
To a terrible rallentando tinkle pass
Across a thumb-hazed sky of plastic glass.
Then you rewind the sea-song that's run down
And paddle in glee, my darling, while I drown.

X. J. KENNEDY

1929–

643

Nude Descending a Staircase

Toe upon toe, a snowing flesh,
A gold of lemon, root and rind,
She sifts in sunlight down the stairs
With nothing on. Nor on her mind.

We spy beneath the banister
A constant thresh of thigh on thigh—
Her lips imprint the swinging air
That parts to let her parts go by.

One-woman waterfall, she wears
Her slow descent like a long cape
And pausing, on the final stair
Collects her motions into shape.

X. J. KENNEDY

644

Last Child

for Daniel

Small vampire, gorger at your mother's teat,
Dubious claim I didn't know I'd staked,
Like boomerangs your cries reverberate
Till roused half-blind, I bear you to be slaked,
Your step-and-fetch-it pimp.
                     Fat lot you care
If meadows fall before your trash-attack,
Streams go to ruin, waste be laid to air.
Will yours be that last straw that breaks earth's back?

Your fingers writhe: inane anemones
A decent ocean ought to starve. Instead
I hold you, I make tries at a caress.
You should not be. I cannot wish you dead.

TED HUGHES

1930–

645

Cat and Mouse

On the sheep-cropped summit, under hot sun,
The mouse crouched, staring out the chance
It dared not take.
          Time and a world
Too old to alter, the five mile prospect—
Woods, villages, farms—hummed its heat-heavy
Stupor of life.
              Whether to two
Feet or four, how are prayers contracted!
Whether in God's eye or the eye of a cat.

646 *Thistles*

Against the rubber tongues of cows and the hoeing hands of
  men
Thistles spike the summer air
Or crackle open under a blue-black pressure.

Every one a revengeful burst
Of resurrection, a grasped fistful
Of splintered weapons and Icelandic frost thrust up

From the underground stain of a decayed Viking.
They are like pale hair and the gutturals of dialects.
Every one manages a plume of blood.

Then they grow grey, like men.
Mown down, it is a feud. Their sons appear,
Stiff with weapons, fighting back over the same ground.

647 *Full Moon and Little Frieda*

A cool small evening shrunk to a dog bark and the
        clank of a bucket—

And you listening.
A spider's web, tense for the dew's touch.
A pail lifted, still and brimming—mirror
To tempt a first star to a tremor.

Cows are going home in the lane there, looping the
        hedges with their warm wreaths of breath—
A dark river of blood, many boulders,
Balancing unspilled milk.

'Moon!' you cry suddenly, 'Moon! Moon!'
The moon has stepped back like an artist gazing
        amazed at a work
That points at him amazed.

648 *Water*

On moors where people get lost and die of air
On heights where the goat's stomach fails

In gorges where the toad lives on starlight
In deserts where the bone comes through the camel's
    nostril

On seas where the white bear gives up and dies of water
In depths where only the shark's tooth resists

At altitudes where eagles would explode
Through falls of air where men become bombs

At the Poles where zero is the sole hearth
Water is not lost, is snug, is at home—

Sometimes with its wife, stone—
An open-armed host, of poor cheer.

P. J. KAVANAGH

1931–

649 *Praying*

As lark ascending
Ending in air
Sings its song there,
If sounds I am sending
Don't go anywhere
I seem not to care.

After singing the lark
Drops back to the ground.
I cover my dark
With the palm of a hand
As horses in fields suddenly stop
Their gallop at a horizon and crop.

SYLVIA PLATH

1932–1963

650   *Frog Autumn*

Summer grows old, cold-blooded mother.
The insects are scant, skinny.
In these palustral homes we only
Croak and wither.

Mornings dissipate in somnolence.
The sun brightens tardily
Among the pithless reeds. Flies fail us.
The fen sickens.

Frost drops even the spider. Clearly
The genius of plenitude
Houses himself elsewhere. Our folk thin
Lamentably.

651   *Barren Woman*

Empty, I echo to the least footfall,
Museum without statues, grand with pillars, porticoes,
      rotundas.
In my courtyard a fountain leaps and sinks back into itself,
Nun-hearted and blind to the world. Marble lilies
Exhale their pallor like scent.

I imagine myself with a great public,
Mother of a white Nikè and several bald-eyed Apollos.
Instead, the dead injure me with attentions, and nothing can
      happen.
The moon lays a hand on my forehead,
Blank-faced and mum as a nurse.

651 Nikè] the goddess of Victory

ADRIAN MITCHELL
1932–

652   *Riddle*

Their tongues are knives, their forks are hands and feet.
They feed each other through their skins and eat
Religiously the spiced, symbolic meat.
The loving oven cooks them in its heat—
Two curried lovers on a rice-white sheet.

JOHN UPDIKE
1932–

653   *Upon Shaving Off One's Beard*

The scissors cut the long-grown hair;
The razor scrapes the remnant fuzz.
Small-jawed, weak-chinned, big-eyed I stare
At the forgotten boy I was.

JAMES SIMMONS
1933–

654   *A Birthday Poem*
for Rachel

For every year of life we light
a candle on your cake
to mark the simple sort of progress
anyone can make,
and then, to test your nerve or give
a proper view of death,
you're asked to blow each light, each year,
out with your own breath.

ANNE STEVENSON

1933–

655

Sous-Entendu

Don't think

that I don't know
that as you talk to me
the hand of your mind
is inconspicuously
taking off my stocking,
moving in resourceful blindness
up my thigh.

Don't think
that I don't know
that you know
everything I say
is a garment.

656

The Demolition

They have lived in each other so long
there is little to do there.
They have taken to patching the floor
while the roof tears.

The rot in her feeds on his woodwork.
He batters her cellar.
He camps in the ruins of her carpet.
She cries on his stairs.

SEAMUS HEANEY

1939–

657

Mother of the Groom

What she remembers
Is his glistening back
In the bath, his small boots
In the ring of boots at her feet.

Hands in her voided lap,
She hears a daughter welcomed.
It's as if he kicked when lifted
And slipped her soapy hold.

Once soap would ease off
The wedding ring
That's bedded forever now
In her clapping hand.

DEREK MAHON

1941–

658

Tractatus

for Aidan Higgins

'The world is everything that is the case'
From the fly giving up in the coal-shed
To the Winged Victory of Samothrace.
Give blame, praise, to the fumbling God
Who hides, shame-facedly, His aged face;
Whose light retires behind its veil of cloud.

The world, though, is also so much more—
Everything that is the case imaginatively.
Tacitus believed mariners could *hear*
The sun sinking into the western sea;
And who would question that titanic roar,
The steam rising wherever the edge may be?

658 Title, l.1] Wittgenstein, *Tractatus Logico-Philosophicus*

NOTES AND REFERENCES

IN this anthology the poets are arranged chronologically according to date of birth, and the poems of each appear in the order in which they were written, in so far as that could be established.

The editors have not invented any titles. First lines are used where no title exists.

None of the poems is an extract. However, we have included self-contained songs from plays, and a few poems from plays, cycles or sequences which naturally separate themselves from the larger context by virtue of a different metre or an individual subtitle.

The spelling and punctuation of all poems before Wordsworth have been modernized, except in cases where alteration would interfere with metre; in medieval poems, a dot over the vowel indicates that it has syllabic value (wordės); elsewhere, the *grave* accent is used to indicated the syllable is either pronounced (as in the uncontracted ending -èd) or receives an unusual stress (envỳ: pronounced en-vie). In the poems of Gerard Manley Hopkins, an acute accent indicates his own system of stress, or 'sprung rhythm'. One post-Wordsworthian exception has been made in that we have modernized the punctuation and use of capitals in Emily Dickinson, a poet who did not write in the expectation of being printed and whose eccentricity in this respect has, we believe, made her work more difficult for many than need be.

The texts have been checked wherever possible against original printed sources, or reliable, scholarly editions, except when the existence of standard modern editions renders this unnecessary. Details of sources (other than those standard modern editions), attribution, or variant readings accepted by us are given in the notes below.

For details of poems in copyright, see the list of Acknowledgements on pp. 279–89.

1–4.	Anonymous. 1. MS Bodley Douce (late 13th c.). 2. MS New College Oxford (late 13th c.). 3. MS BM Royal (early 14th c.). 4. MS Nat. Lib. of Scotland (mid 14th c.). 1, 3, and 4 from *Medieval English Lyrics*, ed. Davies, Faber, 1963. 2 from *The Oxford Book of Medieval English Verse*, ed. Sisam, Oxford University Press, 1970.
7.	Chaucer. Version as *The Oxford Book of Medieval English Verse*, ed. Sisam.
8–14.	Anonymous. 8. MS Copenhagen (mid-15th c.). 9. MS Sloane (mid-15th c.). 10. MS Bodley Douce (mid-15th c.). 11. MS Cambridge Univ. Lib. (late 15th c.). 12. MS BM

Arundel (late 15th c.). **13.** MS BM Add. (early 16th c.). **14.** MS BM Royal App. (early 16th c.). **8, 10, 11, 12, 14** from *Medieval English Lyrics*, ed. Davies, Faber, 1963. **9, 13** from *The Oxford Book of Medieval English Verse*, ed. Sisam, Oxford University Press, 1970.

22.   Baldwin. *The Canticles or Balades of Salomon*, London, 1549.

23.   Anonymous. MS Trinity Coll. Dublin.

24.   Turbervile. *Epitaphs, epigrams, etc.*, 1567, ed. Collier.

25.   Dyer. Version as *At the Court of Queen Elizabeth . . .*, ed. Sargent, Oxford University Press, 1935.

26.   Oxford. Version as *Miscellanies of the Fullers Worthies' Library*, ed. Grosart, 1872.

27–9.   Ralegh. **27.** version as MS Bodley Malone; **28, 29** as Latham ed.

35–43.   Anonymous. From song-books published 1599–1610. **35–7, 39–43.** *English Madrigal Verse*, ed. Fellowes; **38.** Davidson's *Poetical Rhapsody*, 1602.

44.   Harington. *Letters and Epigrams*, ed. McClure, University of Pennsylvania Press, 1930.

46.   Shakespeare. Line 7: 'an edge' as Penguin and other eds.

51.   Davies of Hereford. Fellowes, *English Madrigal Verse*.

52.   Essex. *Miscellanies of the Fullers Worthies' Library*, ed. Grosart.

53.   Bastard. *Poems*, ed. Grosart, 1880.

54.   Nashe. From 'Summer's Last Will and Testament', 1600. *Works*, ed. McKerrow, Blackwell, 1966.

62.   Rowlands. From 'The Poetaster'. *Complete Works*, 1880.

78.   Barnfield. *Poems in Divers Humours*, 1598.

79.   Beedome. *Poems Divine and Humane*, 1641.

80.   Heywood. *Gunaikon* ('The General History of Women'), 1624. Full title 'Upon Ethelburga, Queen of the West-Saxons' (immured in a nunnery as punishment for adultery and murder).

84.   Bristol. In H. Lawes' *Airs and Dialogues*, 1653.

85.   North. *A Forest of Varieties*, 1645.

86.   Phineas Fletcher. *Works*, ed. Grosart, 1869.

87.   Amner. *Sacred Hymns*, 1615.

88–9.   Herbert of Cherbury. *Works*, ed. Moore Smith, 1923. **88.** 'doubtful'.

90–2.   Drummond of Hawthornden. Scottish Text Society, ed. Kastner.

94–100.   Anonymous. 94–6. Fellowes, *English Madrigal Verse*; 97. MS Christ Church; 98. MS BMHarl.; 99. MS Bodley; 100. attrib. Sir Henry Wotton, *Reliquiae Wottoniae*, 1651.

117–19.   Quarles. *Works*, ed. Grosart.

122–3.   Newcastle. 122. from 'The Cavalier and His Lady' . . . ed. Jenkins, Macmillan, 1872; 123. MS BM Add.

132–3.   Shirley. 133. version from *Poems*, 1646.

134.   May. *Epigrams Divine and Moral*, 1633.

135.   Strode. *Works*, ed. Dobell, 1907.

136–8.   Westmorland (Mildmay Fane). ed. Grosart, 1879.

139–41.   Randolph. 140–1. *Poems*, ed. Drury.

142.   Davenant. *The Shorter Poems*, ed. Gibbs, 1972.

146.   Fanshawe. 'Corsica, a wanton nymph: "Our beauty is to us that which to man/Wit is, or strength unto the lion. Then . . ." '

148.   Barksdale. Dedication of Part Three of '*Nympha Libethris* or The Cotswold Muse', 1651.

154.   Montrose. Watson, *Choice Collection of Scots Poems*, 1711.

155.   Bradstreet. *Poems*, ed. Hutchinson, Dover, New York, 1969.

156.   Heath. *Clarastella*, 1650.

157.   Denham. *Poetical Works*, ed. Banks, Anchor, 1969.

158.   Daniel. *Selected Poems*, ed. Stroup, University of Kentucky Press, 1958.

161–2.   Sherburne. *Salmacis*. 1651, reprinted 1819. 162. epigraph from Luke 7:38.

163.   Flecknoe. *Miscellania*, 1653.

165–6.   Newcastle. *Poems and Fancies*, 1653.

167.   Hall. Saintsbury, *Caroline Poets*, ii.

168–9.   Bunyan. 168. *The Pilgrim's Progress*, Part II, 1684; 169. *A Book for Boys and Girls*, 1686.

170.   Philips. Saintsbury, *Caroline Poets*.

173.   Dryden. Addressed to Diana, Mars, and Venus. 1700.

174.   Pain. *Daily Meditations*, ed. Howard, 1936.

176.   Flatman. Saintsbury, *Caroline Poets*, iii.

177.   Dorset (Sackville). *Works*, 1749.

178.   Ayres. Saintsbury, *Caroline Poets*, i.

179–80. Anonymous. **179.** *Miscellany*, 1692; **180.** *Tixall Poetry*, 1813, ed. Clifford.

181. Crowne. *Calisto*, 1675.

182. Rymer. *Curious Amusements*, 1714.

183–6. Rochester. ed. Vieth (**184** and **186** uncertain).

187. Aldrich. Playford, *The Banquet of Music*, 1689.

188. Tate. *Poems*, 1677.

189. Barker. *Poetical Recreations*, 1688.

190. Etherege. *Poems*, ed. Thorpe, Princeton, 1963.

191–2. Winchilsea. *Poems*, ed. Reynolds, Chicago, 1903.

193–4. Walsh. *British Poets*, 1793.

201–2. Lansdowne (Granville). *Poems*, 1732.

208. Smedley. *Poems on Several Occasions*, 1721.

210–11. Johnson. *Poems of Jonathan Swift*, ed. Williams, Oxford, 1958.

215–16. Hill. *Poetical Works*, 1794.

227. Montagu. Dodsley, *A Collection of Poems*, 1775.

228. Wesley. *Poems on Several Occasions*, 1736.

229. Anonymous. Attrib. Wesley in the above.

230. Fitzgerald. *Poems on Several Occasions*, 1733.

231. Dodsley. *Poetical Works*, 1797.

232. Pattison. *Poetical Works*, 1728.

233. Wigson. Shenstone's *Miscellany 1759–63*, ed. Gordon, 1952.

234. Shenstone. *The Gentleman's Magazine*, 1818 (dated Jan. 9th, 1747).

240. Jones. *The Asiatick Miscellany II*, 1786.

248. Blake. 'He who binds' (as most modern eds.).

257. Lamb. *Works*, vol. 3, 'Books for Children', ed. Lucas, 1912; 'probably by Charles', but some eds. attrib. to Mary.

258–63. Anonymous. **258.** no known source other than *Q's Oxford Book of English Verse*; **259.** MS Bodley Rawl. (before 1675); **260.** MS BM Harl. ('King William III to Himself'); **261** (1671) and **262–3** (traditional, modern versions) from *The Oxford Dictionary of Nursery Rhymes*, ed. Opie, 1951.

267–8. Scott. **267.** chapter heading from 'The Bride of Lammermoor'; **268.** 'motto' to 'The Abbot'.

271. Coleridge. l. 6, 'bowl'. Coleridge has 'bole', but it seems unlikely that 'stem' is meant.

274. Southey. 3rd verse by Coleridge.

296–300. Clare. **296, 300.** *Poems,* ed. Tibble, Dent, 1930; **297–9.** *Poems of John Clare's Madness,* ed. Grigson, Routledge and Kegan Paul.

303–8. Emerson. 'Centenary' edition.

325–9. Thoreau. *Collected Poems,* ed. Bode, The Johns Hopkins Press, Baltimore, 1964. **328, 329.** new readings provided by Elizabeth Hall Witherell of *The Writings of Henry D. Thoreau* (in progress), University of California Press, Santa Barbara. **329.** punct. eds.

333. Lowell. *Poetical Works,* vol. 14, Macmillan, 1890.

334–6. Melville. *Works,* vol. 16, Constable, 1924.

337–45. Whitman. ed. Murphy, Penguin, 1975.

348. Cory. *Ionica,* 1905.

349. Allingham. *By the Way: Verses, Fragments, and Notes by William Allingham,* arranged by Helen Allingham, Longmans, Green, and Co., 1912.

353. Patmore. Said to refer to St Margaret's Bay, Kent.

354–5. D. G. Rossetti. *Poetical Works,* ed. Ellis, 1911.

356–65. Dickinson. *Complete Poems,* Faber, 1975. Modernized by J.M. (see introductory note above).

366. C. Rossetti. *Complete Poems,* ed. Crump, Louisiana State University Press, 1979.

367. Lytton. *The Oxford Book of Victorian Verse,* ed. Quiller-Couch, 1912.

391. Coutts. *Selected Poems,* The Bodley Head, 1923.

392. Bourdillon. *Moth-Wings,* 1913.

404–6. Mary Coleridge. *The Collected Poems,* ed. Whistler, Rupert Hart-Davis, 1954.

434–6. Stephen Crane. *Stephen Crane: an Omnibus,* Knopf, 1966.

437–8. Synge. *Poems and Translations,* Allen & Unwin, 1950.

450. Stickney. *Homage to Trumbull Stickney: Poems,* Heinemann, 1968.

468–70. Lindsay. *Selected Poems,* Macmillan, New York, 1965.

474. Freeman. *Collected Poems,* Macmillan, 1928.

476–7. Hulme. *The Life and Opinions of T. E. Hulme,* by A. R. Jones, Gollancz, 1960.

484–5. Wylie. *Collected Poems,* Alfred Knopf, 1938.

521. Owen. *Poems,* ed. Stallworthy, Chatto & Windus, 1985.

ACKNOWLEDGEMENTS

THE editors and publishers gratefully acknowledge permission to repro-
duce the following copyright poems in this book:

Drummond Allison: 'King Lot's Envoys' from *Eight Oxford Poets*,
edited by Sidney Keyes and Michael Meyer. Reprinted by
permission of Routledge & Kegan Paul Plc; 'O Sheriffs' from
The Yellow Night: Poems 1940–1943 (Fortune Press, 1944). Reprinted
by permission of Charles Skilton Ltd.

W. H. Auden: 'Gare du Midi', 'Epitaph on a Tyrant', and 'Base
words are Uttered' Copyright 1940 and renewed 1968 by W. H.
Auden; 'Behold the manly mesomorph' Copyright 1950 by
W. H. Auden; 'At the Party' Copyright © 1965 by W. H. Auden;
'August 1968' Copyright © 1968 by W. H. Auden. All reprinted from
W. H. Auden, *Collected Poems*, edited by Edward Mendelson, by
permission of Faber & Faber Ltd., and Random House, Inc.

George Barker: 'The village coddled in the valley' and 'Epitaph for the
Poet' from *Collected Poems*; 'Not in the poet' from *Villa Stellar*.
Reprinted by permission of Faber & Faber Ltd.

Samuel Beckett: 'Gnome' from *Collected Poems 1930–1978* (1984).
Reprinted by permission of Samuel Beckett, John Calder (Publishers)
Ltd., and Grove Press, Inc.

Hilaire Belloc: 'The Early Morning', 'Discovery', and 'False Heart' from
Complete Verse. Reprinted by permission of Gerald Duckworth & Co.,
Ltd., and A. D. Peters & Co., Ltd.

John Berryman: 'He Resigns' and 'King David Dances' from *Delusions
Etc.* Copyright © 1969, 1971 by John Berryman. Copyright © 1972
by the Estate of John Berryman. Reprinted by permission of Faber &
Faber Ltd., and Farrar, Straus & Giroux, Inc.

John Betjeman: 'Death of King George V' and 'Remorse' from *Collected
Poems*. Reprinted by permission of John Murray (Publishers) Ltd.

Elizabeth Bishop: '*Casabianca*' from *The Complete Poems 1927–1979*.
Copyright © 1983 by Alice Helen Methfessel. Copyright 1936, ©
1979 by Elizabeth Bishop. Reprinted by permission of Farrar, Straus
& Giroux, Inc.

Thomas Blackburn: 'Families' from *Selected Poems*. Reprinted by
permission of Hutchinson Publishing Group Ltd.

ACKNOWLEDGEMENTS

Norman Cameron: 'She and I', 'The Compassionate Fool', 'Forgive Me, Sire', and 'Shepherdess' (from *Three Love Poems*) all in *Collected Poems*. Reprinted by permission of the author's Literary Estate and The Hogarth Press.

Roy Campbell: 'Fishing Boats in Martigues' © Fransisco Campbell Custódio and Ad. Donker (Pty.) Ltd., from *Selected Poems*. Used with permission.

G. K. Chesterton: 'Elegy in a Country Church Yard' and 'Ecclesiastes' from *Collected Poems of G. K. Chesterton*. Copyright 1932 by Dodd, Mead & Company, Inc. Copyright renewed 1959 by Oliver Chesterton. Reprinted by permission of Miss D. E. Collins, A. P. Watt Ltd., and Dodd, Mead & Company, Inc.

Richard Church: 'Be Frugal' from *Collected Poems*. Reprinted by permission of The Estate of Richard Church and Laurence Pollinger Ltd.

John Ciardi: 'Plea' from *In the Stoneworks* (Rutgers University Press, 1961). Reprinted by permission of the author.

Frances Cornford: 'Childhood' and 'All Souls' Night' from *Collected Poems*. Reprinted by permission of Hutchinson Publishing Group Ltd.

Robert Creeley: 'I Know a Man' from *Collected Poems of Robert Creeley 1945–1975*. Reprinted by permission of The University of California Press.

E. E. Cummings: 'Buffalo Bill's' from *Tulips and Chimneys*. Copyright 1923, 1925 and renewed 1951, 1953 by E. E. Cummings. Copyright © 1973, 1976 by the Trustees for the E. E. Cummings Trust. Copyright © 1973, 1976 by George James Firmage. Published in the UK in *Complete Poems 1913–1962* (Granada). Reprinted by permission of Granada Publishing Limited and Liveright Publishing Corporation; 'may my heart always be open to little' Copyright 1938 by E. E. Cummings, renewed 1966 by Marion Morehouse Cummings; 'no time ago' Copyright 1946 by E. E. Cummings; 'Me up at does' Copyright © 1963 by Marion Morehouse Cummings. All from *Complete Poems 1913–1962* and reprinted by permission of Harcourt Brace Jovanovich, Inc., and Granada Publishing Limited.

J. V. Cunningham: 'In Innocence', 'I had gone broke', and 'Interview with Doctor Drink' from *Collected Poems and Epigrams* (Swallow Press, 1971). Reprinted with the permission of The Ohio University Press, Athens, Ohio.

W. H. Davies: 'I am the Poet Davies, William', 'The Villain', 'D is for Dog', and 'All in June' from *The Complete Poems of W. H. Davies*.

ACKNOWLEDGEMENTS

Copyright © 1963 by W. H. Davies. Reprinted by permission of the Executors of the W. H. Davies Estate, Jonathan Cape Ltd., and Wesleyan University Press.

Walter de la Mare: 'Arrogance', 'The Spotted Flycatcher', 'Crazed' and 'The Owl' from *The Complete Poems*. Reprinted by permission of The Literary Trustees of Walter de la Mare and The Society of Authors as their representative.

Alan Dugan: 'Memories of Verdun' from *Collected Poems*. Reprinted by permission of the author and Faber & Faber Ltd.

Clifford Dyment: 'Fox' from *Collected Poems*. Reprinted by permission of J. M. Dent & Sons Ltd.

Richard Eberhart: 'For a Lamb' from *Collected Poems 1930–1976*. Copyright © 1960, 1976 by Richard Eberhart. Reprinted by permission of Chatto & Windus Ltd., and Oxford University Press, Inc.

T. S. Eliot: 'Cousin Nancy' from *Collected Poems 1909–1962*. Copyright 1936 by Harcourt Brace Jovanovich, Inc. Copyright © 1963, 1964 by T. S. Eliot. Reprinted by permission of Faber & Faber Ltd., and Harcourt Brace Jovanovich, Inc.

William Empson: 'Let It Go' from *Collected Poems of William Empson*. Copyright 1949, © 1977 by William Empson. Reprinted by permission of Chatto & Windus Ltd. and Harcourt Brace Jovanovich, Inc.

D. J. Enright: 'The Monuments of Hiroshima' and 'Development' from *Collected Poems*. Reprinted by permission of Watson, Little Ltd.

Gavin Ewart: 'Ending' from *Collected Poems 1933–1980* and 'A 14-Year-Old Convalescent Cat in the Winter' from *The New Ewart: Poems 1980–1982*. Reprinted by permission of Hutchinson Publishing Group Ltd.

Robert D. Fitzgerald: 'Entreaty' from *Forty Years' Poems*. Reprinted by permission of Angus & Robertson UK Ltd.

Ford Madox Ford: '*Sideria Cadentia*: On the Death of Queen Victoria' from *Selected Poems*.

Robert Francis: 'Pitcher' Copyright © 1960 by Robert Francis. Reprinted from *The Orb Weaver* by permission of Wesleyan University Press.

Robert Frost: 'In Neglect', 'A Patch of Old Snow', 'The Cow in Appletime', 'The Line-Gang', 'Dust of Snow', 'Fireflies in the Garden', 'The Armful', 'Were I in Trouble' and 'A Mood Apart' from *The Poetry of Robert Frost*, edited by Edward Connery Lathem. Copyright 1916, 1923, 1928, 1934, 1947, © 1969 by Holt, Rinehart and Winston.

ACKNOWLEDGEMENTS

Copyright 1944, 1951, 1956, 1962 by Robert Frost. Copyright © 1975 by Lesley Frost Ballantine. Reprinted by permission of the Estate of Robert Frost, Jonathan Cape Ltd., and Holt, Rinehart and Winston, Publishers.

Roy Fuller: 'During a Bombardment by V-Weapons' and 'Memorial Poem' ('Week after week, month after month, in pain . . .' is the first of a series entitled *Ten Memorial Poems*) from *Collected Poems*. Both, and 'The Hittites', reprinted by permission of the author.

Robert Graves: 'Flying Crooked', 'At First Sight', 'On Dwelling', 'The Beach', 'Cat-Goddesses', 'In Her Only Way', 'She Is No Liar', and 'In Perspective' from *Collected Poems 1975*. Reprinted by permission of A. P. Watt Ltd., on behalf of the author.

Ivor Gurney: 'After War', 'On the Night', 'The Escape', and 'Moments' from *Collected Poems of Ivor Gurney*, ed. P. J. Kavanagh (1982). Copyright © Robin Haines, Sole Trustee of The Gurney Estate 1982. Reprinted by permission of Oxford University Press.

Seamus Heaney: 'Mother of the Groom' published in the UK in *Wintering Out* and in the USA in *Poems 1965–1975*. Copyright © 1966, 1969, 1972, 1975, 1980 by Seamus Heaney. Reprinted by permission of Faber & Faber Ltd., and Farrar, Straus and Giroux, Inc.

Anthony Hecht: 'Avarice' from 'The Seven Deadly Sins' in *The Hard Hours*. Copyright © 1967 by Anthony E. Hecht. Reprinted by permission of Oxford University Press and Atheneum Publishers, Inc.

Ralph Hodgson: 'The Bells of Heaven' and 'Reason has moons' from *Poems*. Copyright 1917 by Macmillan Publishing Co., Inc., renewed 1945 by Ralph Hodgson. Published in the UK in *Collected Poems*. Reprinted by permission of Mrs Hodgson, Macmillan, London & Basingstoke, and Macmillan Publishing Co., Inc.

A. D. Hope: 'The Bed' from *Collected Poems 1930–1970*. Reprinted by permission of Angus & Robertson UK Ltd.

A. E. Housman: 'Eight o'Clock', 'The night is freezing fast', 'The fairies break their dances', and 'Revolution' Copyright 1922 by Holt, Rinehart and Winston. Copyright 1950 by Barclays Bank Ltd; 'Stars, I have seen them fall', 'Crossing alone the nighted ferry', and 'Half-way, for one commandment broken' Copyright 1936 by Barclays Bank Ltd. Copyright © 1964 by Robert E. Symons. All reprinted from *The Collected Poems of A. E. Housman* by permission of The Society of Authors as the Literary Representative of the Estate of A. E. Housman, Jonathan Cape Ltd., as the British publisher of Housman's *Collected Poems*, and of Holt, Rinehart and Winston, New York.

ACKNOWLEDGEMENTS

Ted Hughes: 'Cat and Mouse' Copyright © 1959 by Ted Hughes, from *Lupercal* (Faber); 'Thistles' Copyright © 1961 by Ted Hughes, and 'Full Moon and Little Frieda' Copyright © 1962 by Ted Hughes, both from *Wodwo* (Faber). These poems are published in the USA in *New Selected Poems* by Ted Hughes (Harper & Row). They are reprinted here by permission of Faber & Faber Ltd., and Harper & Row, Publishers, Inc.

Randall Jarrell: 'The Death of the Ball Turret Gunner' and A War' from *The Complete Poems of Randall Jarrell*. Copyright 1945, 1951 by Mrs Randall Jarrell. Copyright renewed © 1972 by Mrs Randall Jarrell. Reprinted by permission of Faber & Faber Ltd., and Farrar, Straus & Giroux, Inc. 'Well Water' from *The Lost World*. Copyright © Randall Jarrell 1965. Reprinted by permission of Methuen London and Macmillan Publishing Company.

Robinson Jeffers: 'Eagle Valor, Chicken Mind' from *The Double Axe*. © Donnan and Garth Jeffers. Reprinted by permission of Jeffers Literary Properties; 'Ave Caesar', Copyright 1935 and renewed 1963 by Donnan Jeffers and Garth Jeffers, is reprinted from *Selected Poetry of. Robinson Jeffers* by permission of Alfred A. Knopf, Inc.

Elizabeth Jennings: 'Answers' from *Selected Poems* (Carcanet, 1979). Reprinted by permission of David Higham Assoc. Ltd.

Patrick Kavanagh: 'Leave Them Alone' from *Collected Poems* (Granada Publ. Ltd.).

P. J. Kavanagh: 'Praying' from *Selected Poems*. Reprinted by permission of the author and Chatto & Windus Ltd.

X. J. Kennedy: 'Nude Descending a Staircase' and 'Last Child: for Daniel' from *Breaking and Entering*. Copyright © 1961, 1969, 1970, 1971 by X. J. Kennedy. Reprinted by permission of Curtis Brown, Ltd.

Galway Kinnell: 'In a Parlor Containing a Table' from *What Kingdom It Was*. Copyright © 1960 by Galway Kinnell. Reprinted by permission of Houghton Mifflin Company.

Rudyard Kipling: 'A Dead Statesman' from 'Epitaphs of War'; 'Lispeth' ('Look, you have cast out love'), and 'Kidnapped' ('There is a tide') from 'Plain Tales From the Hills'. Copyright 1919 by Rudyard Kipling and reprinted from *Rudyard Kipling's Verse: Definitive Edition* by permission of A. P. Watt Ltd., on behalf of The National Trust for Places of Historic Interest or Natural Beauty, and Macmillan, London, Ltd., and by permission of Doubleday & Company, Inc.

Philip Larkin: 'Home Is So Sad', 'Water', 'Days', and 'As Bad as a Mile' from *The Whitsun Weddings*. Reprinted by permission of Faber & Faber Ltd.

ACKNOWLEDGEMENTS

D. H. Lawrence: 'Piano', 'I Am Like a Rose', 'Glory', 'What Would You Fight For', 'To Women', and 'Intimates' from *The Complete Poems of D. H. Lawrence*, collected and edited by Vivian de Sola Pinto and F. Warren Roberts. Copyright © 1964, 1971 by Angelo Ravagli and C. M. Weekley, Executors of the Estate of Frieda Lawrence Ravagli. Reprinted by permission of Viking Penguin Inc.

Laurie Lee: 'Invasion Summer' from *Selected Poems*. Reprinted by permission of Andre Deutsch and A. D. Peters & Co., Ltd.

C. Day Lewis: 'Where are the War Poets?' from *Collected Poems 1954*. Reprinted by permission of the Executors of the Estate of C. Day Lewis, Jonathan Cape Ltd., the Hogarth Press as publishers, and A. D. Peters & Co., Ltd.

Vachel Lindsay: 'The Leaden-Eyed', 'What the Moon Saw', and 'Factory Windows are Always Broken' from *Collected Poems*. Copyright 1914 by Macmillan Publishing Co., Inc., renewed 1942 by Elizabeth C. Lindsay. Reprinted by permission of Macmillan Publishing Company.

Robert Lowell: 'Lady Ralegh's Lament, 1618' from *For The Union Dead*. Copyright © 1956, 1960, 1961, 1962, 1963, 1964 by Robert Lowell. Reprinted by permission of Faber & Faber Ltd., and Farrar, Straus & Giroux, Inc.

Norman MacCaig: 'Stars and Planets' from *Tree of Strings*. Reprinted by permission of Chatto & Windus.

Hugh MacDiarmid: 'One of the Principal Causes of War' from *The Complete Poems*. Reprinted by permission of Mrs Valda Grieve and Martin Brian & O'Keeffe Ltd.

Patrick MacDonagh: 'No Mean City' from *One Landscape Still* (Secker, 1958).

Phyllis McGinley: 'The Temptations of Saint Anthony' Copyright 1954 by Phyllis McGinley. Copyright renewed © 1982 by Phyllis Hayden Blake; 'The Adversary' Copyright © 1959 by Phyllis McGinley; 'Trinity Place' Copyright 1937 by Phyllis McGinley, copyright renewed ©1965 by Juliet Elizabeth Hayden and Phyllis Hayden Blake. All from *Times Three* and reprinted by permission of Secker & Warburg Limited and Viking Penguin, Inc.

Louis MacNeice: 'Snow', 'The Ear', 'Night Club', 'Precursors', and 'Figure of Eight' from *The Collected Poems of Louis MacNeice*. Reprinted by permission of Faber & Faber Ltd.

Derek Mahon: '*Tractatus*: for Aidan Higgins' from *The Hunt by Night* (1982). © Derek Mahon 1982. Reprinted by permission of Oxford University Press.

ACKNOWLEDGEMENTS

William Meredith: 'Iambic Feet Considered as Honorable Scars' Copyright © 1962 by William Meredith. Reprinted from *The Wreck of the Thresher and Other Poems* by permission of Alfred A. Knopf, Inc.

James Merrill: 'A Renewal' from *Selected Poems*. Copyright © 1961 James Merrill. Reprinted by permission of Chatto & Windus and Atheneum Publishers.

W. S. Merwin: 'When the War is Over' from *The Lice*. Copyright © 1967 by W. S. Merwin. Reprinted by permission of Atheneum Publishers and Harold Ober Associates Incorporated.

James Michie: 'To My Daughter' from *Poems: New and Selected* (1983). Reprinted by permission of the author and Chatto & Windus Ltd.

Edna St Vincent Millay: 'Never May the Fruit Be Plucked', 'To a Young Poet', and 'The True Encounter' from *Collected Poems* (Harper & Row). Copyright 1923, 1939, 1951, 1967 by Edna St Vincent Millay and Norma Millay Ellis. Reprinted by permission.

Adrian Mitchell: 'Riddle' from *Poems*. Reprinted by permission of Jonathan Cape Ltd., on the author's behalf.

Marianne Moore: 'Poetry' Copyright 1935 by Marianne Moore, renewed 1963 by Marianne Moore and T. S. Eliot: 'A Face' Copyright 1951 by Marianne Moore, renewed 1979 by Lawrence E. Brinn and Louise Crane. Both from *Collected Poems* (published in the UK in *The Complete Poems of Marianne Moore*) and reprinted by permission of Macmillan Publishing Co., Inc. and Faber & Faber Ltd; 'I May, I Might, I Must' and 'A Jellyfish' from *The Complete Poems of Marianne Moore*. Copyright © 1959 by Marianne Moore. Both reprinted by permission of Viking Penguin Inc. and Faber & Faber Ltd.

Howard Nemerov: 'An Old Picture', 'A Negro Cemetery Next to a White One', 'The Death of God', and 'Casting' from *Collected Poems* (University of Chicago Press, 1977). Reprinted by permission of the author.

Norman Nicholson: 'Weather Ear' from *The Pot Geranium*. Reprinted by permission of Faber & Faber Ltd., and David Higham Associates Ltd.

Sylvia Plath: 'Frog Autumn' from *The Colossus* (London: Faber/ New York: Knopf). Copyright © 1959 by Sylvia Plath; copyright © Ted Hughes 1967. Reprinted by permission of Olwyn Hughes and Alfred A. Knopf, Inc.; 'Barren Women' from *Collected Poems* (London: Faber/New York: Harper & Row). Copyright © 1981 the Estate of Sylvia Plath. Copyright © Ted Hughes 1981. Reprinted by permission of Olwyn Hughes and Harper & Row Publishers, Inc.

ACKNOWLEDGEMENTS

Ezra Pound: 'The Garden', 'The Lake Isle' from *Personae*. Copyright 1926 by Ezra Pound (published in the UK in *Collected Shorter Poems*). Reprinted by permission of Faber & Faber Ltd. and New Directions Publishing Corporation.

F. T. Prince: 'The Wind in the Tree' reprinted by permission of the author.

John Crowe Ransom: 'Emily Hardcastle, Spinster' Copyright 1924 by Alfred A. Knopf Inc. and renewed 1952 by John Crowe Ransom. Reprinted from *Selected Poems*, Third Edition, Revised and Enlarged, by permission of Alfred A. Knopf, Inc. and Laurence Pollinger Ltd.

James Reeves: 'Double Autumn' from *Subsong* (1969). Reprinted by permission of Heinemann Educational Books Ltd; 'The Stone Gentleman' from *The Password*. Reprinted by permission of William Heinemann Ltd.

Edwin Arlington Robinson: 'Exit' from *The Town Down the River*. Copyright 1910 by Charles Scribner's Sons, renewed 1938 by Ruth Nivison.

W. R. Rodgers: 'Words', 'War-Time', and 'The Lovers' Copyright W. R. Rodgers 1941. Reprinted by permission of Campbell Thompson. & McLaughlin Ltd., on behalf of Lucy Rodgers Cohen.

Theodore Roethke: 'Old Florist' Copyright 1946 by Harper Bros., Inc. 'Dolor' Copyright 1943 by Modern Poetry Association Inc.; 'Night Crow' Copyright 1944 by Saturday Review Association Inc.; 'Wish for a Young Wife' Copyright © 1963 by Beatrice Roethke, Administratrix of the Estate of Theodore Roethke. Reprinted from *The Collected Poems of Theodore Roethke* by permission of Faber & Faber Ltd. and Doubleday & Comapny, Inc.

George Russell (AE): 'Outcast' from *Selected Poems*. Reprinted by permission of Colin Smythe Ltd., on behalf of Mrs Diarmuid Russell.

Carl Sandburg: 'Cool Tombs' from *Cornhuskers*. Copyright 1918 by Holt, Rinehart and Winston, Inc.; Copyright 1946 by Carl Sandburg. Reprinted by permission of Harcourt Brace Jovanovich, Inc.

Siegfried Sassoon: 'Blighters', 'Base Details', 'The General', 'Everyone Sang' and 'In me, past, present, future meet' from *Collected Poems*. Copyright 1918 by E. P. Dutton Co., renewed 1946 by Siegfried Sassoon. Reprinted by permission of George Sassoon and Viking Penguin, Inc.

James Simmons: 'A Birthday Poem: for Rachel' from *The Selected James Simmons*, ed. Edna Langley (Blackstaff, 1978).

286

ACKNOWLEDGEMENTS

C. H. Sisson: 'Money' and 'Easter' © C. H. Sisson from *Collected Poems*, Carcanet New Press, 1984. Used with permission.

Edith Sitwell: 'Bells of Grey Crystal' from *Collected Poems* (Macmillan, 1957). Reprinted by permission of David Higham Associates Ltd.

Stevie Smith: 'The Murderer', 'The Lads of the Village', 'Love Me!' and 'Lady "Rogue" Singleton' from *Collected Poems of Stevie Smith* (Allen Lane/New Directions). Copyright © 1972 by Stevie Smith. Reprinted by permission of James MacGibbon and New Directions Publishing Corporation.

William Jay Smith: 'American Primitive' from *The Traveler's Tree*. Copyright © 1980 by William Jay Smith. By permission of Persea Books, Inc.

Muriel Spark: 'Faith and Works' from *Collected Poems* (Macmillan, London, 1967). First published in *Ladies Home Journal*, May 1965. Copyright © 1965 by Copyright Administration Limited. Reprinted by permission of Harold Ober Associates Incorporated.

Sir John Squire: 'Interior' from *Collected Poems*. Reprinted by permission of Macmillan, London and Basingstoke.

James Stephens: 'A Glass of Beer' from *Collected Poems*. Copyright 1918 by Macmillan Publishing Co., Inc., renewed 1946 by James Stephens. Reprinted by permission of The Society of Authors on behalf of the copyright owner, Mrs Iris Wise, and Macmillan Publishing Company.

Wallace Stevens: 'Anecdote of the Jar' and 'The Death of a Soldier' Copyright 1923 and renewed 1951 by Wallace Stevens; 'Men Made Out of Words' Copyright 1947 by Wallace Stevens. Reprinted from *The Collected Poems of Wallace Stevens* by permission of Faber & Faber Ltd. and Alfred A. Knopf, Inc.

Anne Stevenson: 'Sous-Entendu' and 'The Demolition' from *Travelling Behind Glass: Selected Poems 1963–1973* (1974). © Anne Stevenson. 1974. Reprinted by permission of Oxford University Press.

Arthur Symons: '*Maquillage*', 'At the Cavour', 'Isolation', and 'Venice' in *Collected Poems* (Secker and Warburg, 1924). Reprinted by permission of B. Read.

A. S. J. Tessimond: 'Postscript to a Pettiness' reprinted by permission of Hubert Nicholson, Literary Executor, and Autolycus Publications.

Dylan Thomas: 'On no work of words' and 'Twenty-Four Years' from *The Poems of Dylan Thomas* (Dent/New Directions). Copyright 1939 by New Directions Publishing Corporation, 1953 by Dylan Thomas. Reprinted by permission of David Higham Associates Ltd. and of New Directions Publishing Corporation.

ACKNOWLEDGEMENTS

R. S. Thomas: 'Ire' from *Song At the Year's Turning*. Reprinted by permission of Granada Publishing Ltd.

John Updike: 'Upon Shaving Off One's Beard' Copyright © 1970 by John Updike. Reprinted from *Tossing and Turning* by permission of Alfred A. Knopf, Inc. and André Deutsch. Originally appeared in *The New Yorker*.

Mark Van Doren: 'Good Appetite' from *Collected and New Poems 1925–1963*. Copyright © 1960, 1963 by Mark Van Doren. Reprinted by permission of Hill and Wang, a division of Farrar, Straus & Giroux, Inc.

Vernon Watkins: 'Old Triton Time' reprinted by permission of Gwen Watkins.

Anna Wickham: 'Gift to a Jade' and 'Soul's Liberty' from *Selected Poems*. Reprinted by permission of the author's Literary Estate and Chatto & Windus Ltd.

Richard Wilbur: 'Epistemology' and 'Parable' from *Ceremony and Other Poems*. Copyright 1950, 1978 by Richard Wilbur; 'Piazza di Spagna, Early Morning' and 'Mind' from *Things of This World: Poems of Richard Wilbur*. Copyright © 1956 by Richard Wilbur (all published in the UK in *Poems 1943–1956*); 'The Proof' from *Walking to Sleep: New Poems and Translations*. Copyright © 1964 by Richard Wilbur. All reprinted by permission of Harcourt Brace Jovanovich, Inc. and Faber & Faber Ltd.

William Carlos Williams: 'A Sort of Song' and 'The Hard Listener' from *Collected Later Poems of William Carlos Williams*. Copyright 1944 by William Carlos Williams. Reprinted by permission of New Directions Publishing Corporation.

Judith Wright: 'Portrait' from *Collected Poems 1942–1970*. Reprinted by permission of Angus & Robertson UK Ltd.

W. B. Yeats: 'All Things Can Tempt Me', 'The Cold Heaven' Copyright 1912 by Macmillan Publishing Co., Inc., renewed 1940 by Bertha Georgie Yeats; 'Paudeen' and 'A Coat' Copyright 1916 by Macmillan Publishing Co., Inc., renewed 1944 by Bertha Georgie Yeats; 'A Thought from Propertius' Copyright 1919 by Macmillan Publishing Co., Inc., renewed 1947 by Bertha Georgie Yeats; 'Death', 'Spilt Milk', 'The Choice', and 'Consolation' Copyright 1933 by Macmillan Publishing Co., Inc., renewed 1961 by Bertha Georgie Yeats and Anne Yeats. All the poems are from *W. B. Yeats: The Poems*, edited by Richard J. Finneran (published in the UK in *The Collected Poems of W. B. Yeats*) and are reprinted by permission of Macmillan Publishing Co., Inc. and of A. P. Watt Ltd., for Michael Yeats and Macmillan, London, Ltd.

ACKNOWLEDGEMENTS

Andrew Young: 'In Teesdale', 'A Dead Mole', and 'Ba Cottage' from *Complete Verse*. Reprinted by permission of Secker & Warburg Ltd.

Although every effort has been made to contact copyright owners, we have not always been successful. If notified the publishers will correct any errors or omissions in any future edition.

INDEX OF FIRST LINES

The numbers refer to pages

INDEX OF FIRST LINES

INDEX OF FIRST LINES

INDEX OF FIRST LINES

INDEX OF AUTHORS

The numbers refer to pages

INDEX OF AUTHORS